Big Data

A Guide to Big Data Trends, Artificial Intelligence, Machine Learning, Predictive Analytics, Internet of Things, Data Science, Data Analytics, Business Intelligence, and Data Mining

Contents

Introduction

Unless you have been asleep over the past decade, you have noticed that data is becoming increasingly important in society. Large amounts of data are being collected about virtually everything, and computers are being used to sift through the data and analyze it. Perhaps the most immediately recognizable application of this is in the realm of commerce and finance. Big data is used to determine your likes and dislikes and show you appropriate advertising as you go about using the internet or your mobile phone. Big data is what powers social media sites like Facebook, which use it to show content you may be interested in besides the ever-present targeted advertising.

In the financial world, big data has replaced the banker or loan officer. It is used to determine whether you are a good credit risk. Big data is also being used by the police force, which is attempting to learn new ways to track criminals. Many have suggested that big data could be used to predict the risk of a given individual becoming a mass shooter in the future. In short, the applications of big data are practically endless.

The secret to big data is machine learning. Briefly, this involves letting computers look at the data and find relationships between different elements and patterns that human observers could not possibly figure out on their own. This is true simply because we cannot go through all the reams of data using our slow human minds and analyze it for hidden patterns in the data the way a computer can.

The potential applications of big data are endless and varied. They range from the trivial to the dangerous. In a totalitarian society, there is no telling how big data would be used. Indeed, in some countries, it is already being used for various types of surveillance that many find uncomfortable. For example, in China, big data has been used to give every citizen a "social score," and people with low social scores have certain restrictions placed on them, such as travel restrictions.

On a more positive note, many corporations are using big data to become more efficient, including several airlines. Big data is particularly useful in the area of logistics, where it has been applied to find areas in a company's operations that are wasting time, money, and fuel.

In this book, we will investigate big data from a bird's-eye view, covering the subject from a beginner's perspective and introducing its many applications. This will include not only mundane topics like targeted advertising but also an exploration of machine learning and artificial intelligence. Many of the applications of big data have been incorporated into business intelligence and data analytics, and in the process of data mining. These topics will be investigated in this book.

Chapter 1: What Is Big Data?

Big data. It is all over the media, and it seems like everyone is talking about it. Pundits, websites, and news anchors are constantly mentioning "big data," but it is never precisely defined. What is big data, exactly, and why should you care about it?

As we will see, big data is one of the most potent and surprising trends of the twenty-first century. While people have been focused on their smartphones, lost in texting and playing games, big data has been working behind the scenes, revealing patterns and information in ways that would have been thought to be virtually impossible in past decades. Big data can have both positive and negative applications. Many people view big data as a privacy threat, and they have a point; however, big data is also helping companies become more efficient, delivering more value to customers while saving money at the same time.

Nobody knows where the future will lead—but one thing we do know is that big data will play a part in it. Anyone who wants an awareness of where we are headed should be familiar with big data.

Let us create a basic working definition of big data. You can think of it as large amounts of what appears to be random data collected on people or activities in a wide variety of circumstances. Regarding people, this will include data on where you are shopping, what websites you are visiting, where you are traveling, what products you are purchasing, and so forth. This data could also be collected on any activity related to a business or organization. It could be data collected by UPS on the habits and fuel use of their drivers, or data collected by government agencies related to criminal activity or an epidemic.

The data by itself is useless. It must be analyzed, and computers, directed by experts called data scientists, are used to find hidden patterns, associations, and trends that may exist in the data. Corporations, governments, and other large organizations are using big data to seek out information on human behavior relevant to their operations, whether that involves improving their own efficiency, delivering better services, or developing new products that their customer base will want.

Where Did Big Data Come from and What Does It Mean?

The first thing to note about big data is that we live in an era of data collection. This started long ago, as soon as people could begin keeping records. Keeping records on stone tablets or even with pen and paper is not very efficient. You might have a wealth of data collected within your pile of papers but cannot readily analyze or explore it. If human beings tried doing this, centuries would pass before much information was extracted from the data.

In the twentieth century, that began to change with the invention of electronic computers. Again, at first there were many inefficiencies. In the early days of computing data, the collection was inefficient and limited. Computers had limited memory capacity, and relative to today's machines, they were very slow.

Nonetheless, once corporations and governments were able to do so, keeping collections of data became increasingly common. As time has passed, the amount of data and the varied types of data that have been collected and maintained has been continually growing. Even in the 1930s, the government began tracking people with the issuance of social security numbers. That pales in comparison to what is known today. In the modern world, your social security number is associated with a huge amount of data. Financial companies can use it to access lots of information about your history and decide in seconds if they are willing to give you a loan or not.

The key to data is that it contains hidden patterns, which are not immediately recognizable. However, computers—doing what they do best—can go through reams of data, analyze it, and find hidden patterns that nobody ever imagined existed.

This has allowed businesses and other entities to solve problems that could not have been solved in the past. One of the most famous examples is Southwest Airlines. By having computers sift through the reams of data it had collected, they were able to determine that airplanes in their fleet were wasting large amounts of fuel idling on the tarmac. Once the problem had been identified—and it was something that no human had ever thought about—it could be rectified. The airline claims it has saved hundreds of millions of dollars by making changes after the problems were identified.

Another area where big data has had a large impact is in the area of finance, as we have already alluded to. Banks have been collecting huge amounts of data, and there is data on everything you do regarding money. Your entire financial history is available—everything you have shopped for, every loan that you have ever taken out, and so on.

The amazing thing about big data, which we will talk about in more detail later on, is that machine learning has allowed computers to learn things from the data that have massively increased the efficiency of various computer systems such as determining whether someone is a good credit risk or not. In many cases, surprises abound. In other words, you could make simple rules based on common sense, for example, looking to see how many late payments they have had. The power of big data is that when the computer uses machine learning to sift through large amounts of information, it can find connections or patterns in the data that nobody would have known existed. Now I do not have ready access to the data used to determine whether someone should get a loan, so we will have to make up some examples to give you an idea of the kinds of things that could be found by looking for patterns in the data. Our example will be highly exaggerated to make the point.

For example, the computer might find that people who were born in the month of August in the zip code 88888 are three times as likely, when compared to the average, to default on auto loans. Banks could then use this information to require people born in August in that zip code to have higher standards than average to qualify for the loan. These decisions are made in seconds, and someone from that zip code might feel bewildered when they are rejected for the loan. This is a game of probability, so the decision may be wrong or right for any given individual, but it will be the right decision for the bank, in the aggregate.

The Facebook lookalike audience is an excellent example of the real-world power of big data. If you have never done Facebook advertising, you may not be aware of the lookalike audience. Sometimes you are being shown ads for things you are interested in—not because they have any data about you directly related to the ad itself—but because you share certain characteristics with other people who have purchased the product.

Let us take an example. Those advertising products that teach people how to train their own dog at home have collected reams of data. In fact, Facebook and other companies have data on their computer drives of people who have already purchased such products in the past.

It turns out that people who are likely to purchase such a product will have many shared characteristics. The data must be analyzed to determine what those characteristics are, and not knowing what they are, we can certainly propose that there will probably be some surprises. The specific characteristics are completely irrelevant, however. Facebook will analyze the data to find the characteristics. It will then search its general audience and find other people who have not yet purchased such a product but have the same characteristics. Who knows what it is? Maybe they are of a certain age and gender, have a certain income or education level, or they are more likely to reside in certain areas of the country.

Facebook will then use that information to create a lookalike audience for the advertiser. Then the advertiser shows their ads to these people, knowing that they are extremely likely to purchase the product, based on whatever characteristics Facebook has discovered. This is all automatic, and the computer does it completely. The people identified start-seeing ads for the product they are likely to buy, and, guess what—they will buy the product at very high conversion rates compared to the norm in sales.

Big Data Key Number One: Volume

The first key to big data is the word *big*. Yes, that means volume. To have big data so you can spot previously unknown patterns in the data, you must collect large amounts or volumes of data. Generally speaking, the more data, the better.

This has been one of the biggest changes in recent decades. Since the mid-1990s, data storage capacity has become dirt cheap. Cloud computing allows virtually unlimited storage of data, and it is readily accessed. Faster internet connections and CPU speeds have all translated into being able to access massive amounts of data at incredible speeds and then analyzing that data and find out new things.

The main factor to gain the volume necessary to glean this kind of information has been the massive reduction in costs required to store data, retrieve it, and do computations on that data.

Big Data Key Number Two: Variety

Big data now comes in many forms. You are leaving trails all over the place, and anyone who has access to all these different streams of data might be able to find amazing bits of information. The data is large and unstructured, but it contains hidden information that will prove useful in some context. The amazing variety of data available is endless. For example, you might have a grocery shoppers' card that entices you by offering discounts. Guess what? That card is being used to track every little thing you purchase. If you are sneaking off to the store every night to buy alcohol, somebody knows about this somewhere.

There are also large amounts of data about what videos you choose to watch on YouTube, and what news sites you visit and how often. There is also data on what other types of websites you are using.

All these varied bits of data can be combined into useful information. In fact, as we mentioned above, some have suggested that this data could be used to estimate someone's risk of committing a mass shooting. It is hard to know if this is true or not, but there is a solid chance that it would work, at least in some cases. People prone to that kind of violence are certainly likely to be watching certain videos, visiting specific kinds of websites, and probably shopping online for weapons. The risk is that sometimes the big data won't be completely accurate, so when legal issues are involved, significant mistakes could target innocent people. You have probably noticed that while at times the products being shown to you in advertisements are downright spooky, as if they were reading your mind, sometimes they are a definite miss. Using big data in law enforcement must be treated with care.

Variety in collected data spans many different types of information. For example, it is at least possible to scan license plates. This information could be used to determine your whereabouts and travel habits. Since nearly everyone is carrying a smartphone around with them, the information cellular companies are collecting could reveal your movements over any time period someone wished to investigate.

Big Data Key Number Three: Velocity

Velocity refers to the speed of data movement and processing. The velocity of data processing has increased dramatically over the last three decades. The movement to flash memory and larger memory capacity, in general, has accelerated the increase in velocity. Now data can be processed nearly in real-time. This magnifies the power of big data enormously.

Big Data Key Number Four: Value

Value refers to the inherent value present in all data. At first, data is just loose collections of bits of information. Without being analyzed, it will not be immediately clear what patterns the data contains and who it will be useful to, but one thing you can guarantee is that some value is in the data. To find that value, will require effective analysis, not just by computers but by professional data scientists who know how to ask the right questions about the data and interpret the information they get back from their computer systems.

The power of social media companies is a practical consequence of this. By collecting huge amounts of data on people's habits, Facebook has positioned itself as an extremely valuable company that can provide advertisers and others with data that has a huge predictive value. It also allows advertisers to target audiences with laser point precision.

In the medieval world, gold was the highest object of value. In the nineteenth century, oil became known as "black gold." In today's world, data can be described as the new gold. Data has power, and any company that has it in their possession is wealthy indeed.

Big Data Key Number Five: Veracity

This is the last big data key, rounding out what is known as the "five v's" in the field of data science. Veracity refers to how accurate the data is and how reliably it can be trusted. Many things influence the veracity of any data set, and statistical bias is one important factor. Smaller data sets are more likely to be statistically biased, which is one reason volume is an important factor in big data. Increasing the volume of data increases the probability that the data is less statistically biased. That also increases its value. Data veracity is also influenced by many other factors, such as security. People often think about data being hacked and having their privacy exposed, or perhaps they will suffer from identity theft. These problems are important in their own right, but the reverse could also occur. The data could be corrupted, perhaps without the knowledge of those who hold and use it.

A Brief History of Big Data

As mentioned before, human beings have always collected various types of data. One thing they have lacked is the ability to consolidate data effectively and the inability to analyze it. So how and when did these abilities develop?

The first break in the processing of data came with the invention of the Hollerith tabulating machine, which used punch cards to encode and represent data. This was a mechanical device, but in reality, the principles behind it are the same principles used in digital computers. The U.S. government spurred the invention, which has been collecting census data on the population since the founding of the country. When the country was small, collecting this information and tabulating it by hand was relatively feasible. By the late nineteenth century, it was becoming increasingly cumbersome. It was estimated that it would take nearly nine years to tabulate the results of the 1880 census. Since the government was doing a census every ten years, having the last one finish only a year before the next one would be completely absurd. Not to mention that by the time the data was tabulated, it would be out-of-date information. This prompted Hollerith to invent his tabulating machine, which reduced the amount of time required to process the data to a few months. It was a truly revolutionary development. Punch cards, by the way, were eventually used in the first digital computers, and they were used well into the 1970s.

The next major step was taken in 1927 when a German engineer figured out how to store information on a magnetic tape. This was a remarkable invention that would make it much easier to store and read data electronically. The use of magnetic devices to store and retrieve data is still popular, although computers are moving from traditional hard drives to flash drives. Think about your credit or debit cards, which still store information on magnetic strips.

The next big development was the invention of the electronic computer. The first computers were large and did not have that much computing power by today's standards. These were used in World War II mainly to crack codes used by Nazi Germany. They were also used for early calculations that had military applications, such as computing projectile trajectories that had to be calculated by hand otherwise. The move from the mechanical processing and storage of data to the electronic processing of data was truly revolutionary. The power of the computer exponentially increased, and processing times and data storage capabilities were as well. It would still be many decades before this would start taking off, but there was no looking back at this point.

By the mid-1960s, the idea of big data started to come to the surface. The U.S. government led the way, with the idea of storing people's fingerprints. And you will not be surprised to learn that the U.S. government wanted to start storing tax information about people on computers.

The 1960s also saw another major development that would not come to full light until the early to mid-1990s. This was the invention of the internet. In those days, it was called Arpanet and its purpose was to allow the U.S. government to continue functioning in the event of a nuclear attack. The idea was to distribute computing power and data, rather than having it centralized at one location where it could be easily destroyed. By having a distributed network, the data could be always available as long as the total network was not completely destroyed.

Another important development that began in the late 1950s was the development of machine learning and artificial intelligence. For decades, the field of artificial intelligence made big promises while delivering little in the way of results, but it is starting to pay off in today's world. The marriage of machine learning to data has made big data and its results possible.

The invention of the personal computer was also an important step in the evolution of big data. Suddenly, by the mid-1980s, computers were found in almost every business. At the time, the user interfaces and storage capacity were laughably limited, but the growth of computers and their acceptance by businesses would make big data inevitable, as soon as the technology caught up to a point to be able to collect and analyze the data.

When the Cold War ended, this concept was expanded to civilian life to become the internet. A British computer scientist who was working at the CERN physics laboratory in Switzerland came up with the idea of HTML and the World Wide Web. CERN gave worldwide access to the network, and the modern internet was born.

Processing Power, Ubiquitous Computing, and Storage

After the turn of the twenty-first century, computing power and storage capacity continued to increase. As time goes on, there has been less development in the speed and power of CPU chips; however, other aspects of computing power have increased exponentially. The main developments in this area have been cloud computing, massive improvements in memory capacity, and speed in moving data from one place to another. It was not until 2005 and onward that the modern concept of big data had real meaning. About this time corporations became consciously aware of the amount of data being generated as a result of people using the internet. Data of all kinds were being generated—from what people were searching for on Google, to the videos watched on YouTube, and what people were shopping for online. At that time, Facebook had barely come into existence and gained popularity.

This capacity is only set to increase. People have been waiting for the arrival of a new bit of hype, the so-called "Internet of Things." This is an imagined future where appliances of various kinds—from your refrigerator to your toilet—are connected to the internet. This imagined future sees every device that people use collecting data, which can then be used by corporations to analyze behavior and habits down to the last detail. This would help companies operate with higher levels of efficiencies and presumably better meet consumer needs. Early stages of this are seen with devices like Alexa and with digital television and services like Roku, Netflix, and Apple TV that can collect data on what people are watching.

A smart refrigerator connected to the internet could analyze the food in your refrigerator and recommend future shopping lists, contact the grocery store to alert them that you need certain items, or even order the items for you. People have imagined smart toilets that could monitor users for health indicators in real time and communicate this information to their doctor.

Hadoop and Spark

Hadoop and Spark are open-source frameworks used to store, analyze, and process large amounts of data. Hadoop is a java framework that breaks down a task into smaller parts and then passes down components of the task to sets of computers that do the actual processing. Spark is a data processing engine, which can work on big data. Spark is designed to work faster than Hadoop. The importance of these tools is they made big data easier and cheaper to handle and process.

Privacy Concerns

The idea of the Internet of Things, where there is more and more direct analysis of what people are doing, has raised many privacy concerns. Already, companies like Facebook, Google, and Amazon are on the defensive regarding privacy concerns, with governments the world over investigating how they are handling privacy. With that in mind, it is not entirely clear where the Internet of Things is headed; privacy concerns might limit its applicability or, at the very least, regulate what can be done with the data. Only time will tell how this will develop, but the ability to connect all your appliances to the internet and analyze data from them has definitely arrived.

The Benefits of Big Data

Regarding large organizations like corporations and governments, big data provides many benefits. Let us focus on some of the positives for the government that also benefit the populace. One use of big data already finding application is using it to allocate police resources more efficiently. It has been used to study criminal behavior over time in various cities and has revealed patterns in criminal data that were previously unknown to law enforcement officials. This has allowed them to address staffing issues far more efficiently so they will have the most efficient number of officers on duty at the right times. In addition, big data has allowed police departments to learn the best locations to put police forces, not only based on what is a high crime area and what isn't, but also regarding other factors that might indicate when and where criminal activity could occur, such as the weather, time of year, or day of the week.

Big data is also helping with the science of epidemiology. It is improving the ability of organizations like the Centers for Disease Control to predict the course of an epidemic. By looking for patterns in data collected from past epidemics, computer systems can assist health officials in working with local governments to contain the spread of epidemics, allocate resources, and assist with other activities.

Hospitals are also becoming more efficient using big data. One way this is working is in managing the nursing staff. Some hospitals have been able to track the locations of nursing staff at all time, and the results from analyzing the data have helped them allocate nurses more efficiently where they are needed the most. Applications of big data have also helped with seemingly mundane things like hand washing by hospital staff, which can have a big impact on containing the spread of infectious diseases. Every branch of government is using big data at all levels to improve efficiency and cut costs. The applications are so numerous that we can mention a few.

Regarding corporations, the benefits of big data are hard to overstate. We have already touched on its use to increase the efficiency and conversion rates of advertising. Models based on big data are also being used to anticipate consumer demand in the future, to increase the efficiency of delivering services, and develop products that the consumer base is likely to enjoy and find useful. The impact of big data on the operation of large corporations has only started to be felt in the past five years or so. There is no telling how this will benefit large corporations going forward. It has also had a major impact in creating new career paths (data scientist) and making information the gold of the twenty-first century. The most valuable companies are those who have the data, and that is not likely to change despite rumblings from the European Union and the U.S. Congress trying to control the tech giants.

As we demonstrated in the case of Southwest Airlines, one of the more useful applications of big data has been in the area of logistics and company efficiency. Many companies like UPS are using big data to slash costs and improve reliability. These types of efficiencies are not awe-inspiring in the same way that something like the Internet of Things might be, but improved corporate efficiency is helping to eliminate fuel waste, enable companies to deliver packages at fast rates, and make the production of manufactured goods far more efficient.

Detection of fraud and compliance is another area where big data is being utilized. This is done by all the major banks and by taxing authorities like the Internal Revenue Service. Internet security is another area related to fraud where big data is having a big impact.

Commercially, big data is used to develop a more personalized delivery of goods and services. We have already mentioned the use of big data for highly targeted advertising. This trend will only gather in strength as time goes on. Despite privacy concerns, the benefits to companies large and small are too large, and that is likely to win the day.

Another area where big data will likely grow in importance is in the area of predictive analytics. Using pattern detection when analyzing old data before failures, combined with machine learning, the hope is that smart systems can detect future failures by recognizing when patterns exist that have indicated a coming failure in the past. Interestingly, this idea was anticipated in the 1960s novel *2001: A Space Odyssey*, when the HAL 9000 computer anticipated a future failure of a communications device on the spaceship. Incidentally, the computer turned out to be wrong in its prediction, which was quite shocking for the characters in the novel.

While people have been focused on the obvious benefits of technology and imagining a future filled with robots, rapid travel, and perfect health, big data is turning out to be one of the most important things to spring from the computer revolution that took place during the mid-to-late twentieth century. Everyone agrees that big data is here to stay, and its use and applications are just beginning. In the next chapter, we will introduce the concept of data science and investigate future trends in big data.

Chapter 2: Big Data Trends and Data Science

In this chapter, we will investigate the field of data science and then look at current trends in big data and where they might be heading. No matter what you think about big data, one thing we know for sure is that it is not going away any time soon.

What Is Data Science?

As the importance of big data has grown, a new field has emerged for scientists/engineers who are specialists in working with big data. This field is known as data science. It is an interdisciplinary field, combining statistics and probability with computer science and business acumen. The field is in high demand, and it is expected that in the coming years that demand will only increase.

In short, the role of a data scientist is to interpret and choose things of value from big data. They will use many tools to assist them in this process, and computing power will be an important part of that. While much attention is focused on machine learning and artificial intelligence, in the end, the data scientist and the interpretive analysis of the human mind play a central role in the value of big data.

Since computers are at the heart of big data and the analytics used on it, some background in computer science and/or computer engineering will be fundamental to the field of data science. Programming skills are necessary, but that does not mean a practitioner of data science must be an advanced computer scientist or get a PhD in the field. In fact, compared to that level, the kind of programming most data scientists do is a bit rudimentary. However, you can go further in certain areas if you have more expertise in hot topics like machine learning.

Statistics and probability perform a central function in the field of data science. That is the nature of this game. When you have large amounts of data, the analysis of the data will naturally be statistical. People won't be doing this by pencil and paper, but a data scientist needs a thorough understanding of statistics and the application of many mathematical models such as linear regression. This will help the data scientist develop the right models used to look for patterns in data and build models used for machine learning.

It is also important for data scientists to have some business acumen. Again, this is an interdisciplinary field, so you don't need an MBA or anything like that. Some understanding of business operations, marketing, logistics, and other issues make a data scientist more useful to large corporations, like manufacturers or airlines that may be looking to use data scientists.

To see why data science and big data is necessary, visualize having direct access to the kind of data we are talking about. It could be listed in a comma-separated file or a spreadsheet. If you opened such a file, it would look almost like gibberish. You might see columns of names and numbers, and you could scroll up and down and left and right trying to make sense of it, which would be virtually impossible. This is why computing power must be applied to big data. Going through reams of data to find patterns contained in it is a task perfectly suited for computers.

You cannot just feed computer data and expect answers to pop out like magic. The data scientist uses certain tools and mathematical models to tease out the information. The initial judgment of the data scientist will get things started, as he will choose the best method to analyze the data. Many data scientists write programs in Python, a simple interpretive language, to analyze big data. They can also use a statistical package called R. If the data is stored in a formal database, then SQL, a language used to sort and pull data from large databases, can be used as part of the process.

Data scientists may do testing by using different machine learning algorithms and methods to get the most out of the data. It is important to avoid being led astray. Unfortunately, that possibility always exists, and it is always possible to draw the wrong conclusions from a set of data.

Later, we will explore the role of machine learning in data science. It turns out that machine learning is playing a more central role in data science and the evaluation of big data. This is a different type of approach, whereby, rather than giving computer-specific instructions to execute, you let the computer learn on its own by presenting it with large data sets. For working with big data, the computer can be trained on small subsets of data. Once the data scientist is satisfied with the level of learning the computer has achieved, it can then be unleashed on the big data, where it can search for the patterns and relationships of interest for the application being investigated.

Trends in Big Data

As we move into the third decade of the twenty-first century, several new trends in big data may take hold. The first is the streaming of data combined with machine learning. Traditionally, computers have learned from data sets that were fed to computer systems in a controlled fashion. Now the idea is developing to use data streaming in real time, so computer systems could learn as they go. It remains to be seen if this is the best approach, but combining this with the Internet of Things, there is a big hope for massive improvements in accuracy, value, and efficiency regarding big data.

Another important trend in the coming years is sure to be the increasing role of artificial intelligence. This has applications across the board, with simple things like detecting spam email all the way to working robots that many fears will destroy large numbers of jobs that only require menial labor. The belief among those familiar with the industry is that despite decades of slow progress regarding artificial intelligence, its time has definitely arrived. It is expected to explode over the next decade. Recently, robots have been unveiled that can cook meals in fast-food restaurants, work in warehouses unloading boxes and stacking them on shelves, and everyone is talking about the possibilities of self-driving cars and trucks.

Businesses are eager to take advantage of AI as it becomes more capable and less expensive. It is believed that applications of artificial intelligence to business needs will increase company efficiency exponentially. In the process, tedious and time-consuming tasks, both physical-related tasks like unloading boxes at a warehouse and data-related tasks done in offices, will be replaced by artificially intelligent systems and robotics. The movement in this direction is already well underway, and some people are fretting quite a bit over the possibility of millions of job losses. However, one must keep in mind that revolutionary technology has always caused large numbers of job losses, but this impact is only temporary because the freed labor and productive capacity have resulted in the creation of new jobs and industries that nobody anticipated before. One example of this is the famous Luddites who protested mechanical looms that manufactured textile goods in the eighteenth century. They rioted and destroyed many factories when these early machines were introduced. However, by the end of the century, literally ten times as many people were working in the same industry because of the increased productivity provided by the introduction of machines. It remains to be seen, but one can assume this is likely to happen yet again.

Cloud computing has played a central role in the expansion of big data. Hybrid clouds are expected to gain in the coming years. A hybrid cloud will combine a company's own locally managed and controlled data storage with cloud computing. This will help increase flexibility while enhancing the security of the data. Cloud bursting will be used, where the company can use its own local storage until surges in demand force it to use the cloud.

One up-and-coming issue related to big data is privacy. Privacy concerns are heightening, with people becoming more aware of the ubiquitous targeted advertising that many companies are using. In addition, large-scale hacks of data are continually making the news, and consumers are becoming increasingly concerned about what companies like Facebook and Amazon are doing with their data. As mentioned in the first chapter, the Internet of Things is one of the next big things coming in the tech revolution; however, people may be leery of such developments given recent trends and issues surrounding privacy. If people are concerned with Facebook invading their privacy, they will certainly be concerned about their toilet, electric meter, and refrigerator collecting data on their activities and sending it who knows where. Politicians the world over are also getting in on the act, with calls for regulation of big tech companies coming from both sides of the Atlantic.

Many people are anticipating with excitement the implementation of 5G cellular networks. This is supposed to result in much faster connection speeds for mobile devices. The capacity for data transfer is expected to be much larger than is currently available. 5G networks are claimed to have download speeds that are ten times as great compared with 4G cellular networks. This will increase not only the speed of using the internet on a mobile device but also the ability of companies to collect data on customers in real time, and possibly integrating streaming data from 5G devices with machine learning.

A 5G connection will also allow you to connect more devices simultaneously. This could be helpful for the advent of the Internet of Things described earlier. At the time of writing, 5G is barely being tentatively rolled out in select cities like Chicago.

One anticipated trend in the next few years will be that more companies will make room for a data curator. This is a management position that will work with data, present data to others, and understand the types of analysis needed to get the most out of big data.

Past Trends and Their Continuation

In the past, the biggest factors influencing the growth of big data have included increasing the processing power of computer chips, increasing storage capacity, both of individual computers and cloud computing, cheaper memory with a much larger capacity, and increasing broadband speeds. While the famous "Moore's Law" is often cited with the doubling of processor speed and capacity every two years, it is clear that, at some point, this progress will slow down. In fact, the evidence indicates that, as far as increasing speed and capacity of computer chips is concerned, there is already a slowdown. Over the coming years, we can continue to expect to see increased performance and capacity, but the progress seen over the past two decades is likely to start slowing down.

One wildcard in developing big data is the possible invention of devices governed by quantum computation rather than classical computers. Quantum computation can make its presence felt in many ways if it becomes a reality. One area it will likely impact is the development of totally secure communications. It might also be able to produce computers that can process data at much higher and faster rates as compared to conventional or classical computers. It is important to understand that quantum computation would be a *revolutionary* and not evolutionary change. However, many practical difficulties might prevent quantum computation from ever being anything more than a theory. At this time, it remains to be seen whether it will become a practical reality.

Chapter 3: Type of Big Data

Data can come in many forms. It might be in the form of location data created from cell phone pings, a listing of all the YouTube videos you have ever watched, or all the books you have purchased on Amazon. Often, it is desirable to integrate different types of data into a single coherent picture. Data might be used in real time or could be analyzed later to find hidden patterns.

In this chapter, we will explore the general types or classes of big data. As we will see, big data can come in the form of structured or unstructured data. Moreover, it can come from different sources. Understanding the types of big data will be important for getting a full understanding of how big data is processed and used.

Structured Data

Structured data is the kind of data you would expect to find in a database. It can include stored items such as dates, names, account numbers, and so forth. Data scientists can often access structured data using SQL. Large amounts of structured data have been collected over decades.

Structured data can be human-generated, such as people entering payment information when ordering a product, or it could be data entered manually by people working at a company. If you apply for a loan and fill out an online form, this is human-generated data, which is also structured data. This data would include an entry that could be put in a database with name, social security number, address, place of employment, and so on.

In today's world, structured data is also computer-generated without the involvement of any people. When data is generated by computer systems, it might be of a different character than that described above, but it can still be structured data. For example, if your cell phone company was tracking you, you could create data points that had your GPS coordinates, together with the date and time. Additional information like your name or customer identifier used by the cell phone company could also be included.

Other structured data can include tracking websites. As you are using your computer, your activity could be tracked, and the URL, date, and time could be recorded and stored as structured data.

Traditionally, structured data has been stored in relational databases and accessed using a computer language paired with SQL. However, these tools are in the midst of an evolving process as they adapt to the world of big data. The reason things are changing is that many types of data, drawn from different sources, are finding their way together into the same bits of structured data.

For those who have little familiarity with relational databases, you can think of an entry in a database having different fields. We can stick to the example of an application for a loan as an example. It will have first and last name fields with pre-determined character lengths. The first name field might be ten characters and the last name field might be twenty characters. We are just providing these values as examples; whoever designs the database will make them long enough to be able to record data from most names.

When collecting information for a financial application, date of birth and social security number will be collected. These will be given specific formats in the database, with a date field and a character field that is eleven characters wide to collect the social security number.

We could go on describing all the fields, but I think you get the point of how the data is structured. With structured data, specific pieces of information collected, and the formats of the information, are pre-defined. Each data point collected is called a field, and every element in the database will have the same fields, even if the person neglects to fill out some of the data.

Batch processing of structured data can be managed using Hadoop.

Unstructured Data

A lot of big data is classified as unstructured data. This encompasses a wide variety of data that comes from many sources. One example of unstructured data is spam email. Machine learning systems have been developed to analyze email to estimate whether its spam. The data in this case is the text included in the message, the subject line, and possibly the email address and sending information for the message. While there are certain common phrases used in spam emails, someone can type an email with any text they please, so there is no structure at all to the data. Think about this in terms of a database. As we mentioned above, a database has fields that are specific data types and sizes, and structured data will include specific items collected with the data.

Another example of unstructured data could be text messages. They are of varied length and may contain different kinds of information. Not only could a person enter in numerical or alphabetic/textual information, but images, emojis, and even videos can be included. Any randomly selected text message may have one or all these elements or some value in between. There is no specific structure to the data, unlike an entry in a relational database.

Similar to text messages, posting on social media sites is unstructured data. One person might type a plain text message, while someone else might type a text message and include an image. Someone else might include many emojis in their message, and another posting might include a video.

Often, unstructured data is analyzed to extract structured data. This can be done with text messages or postings on social media sites to glean information about people's behaviors.

There are many kinds of unstructured data. For example, photographs and surveillance data—which includes reams of video—are examples of unstructured data.

Semi-Structured Data

Data can also be classified as semi-structured. This is data that can have structured and unstructured elements together.

Storing Data

As mentioned earlier, structured data is stored in relational databases. In the 1990s, this was the primary storage mechanism of big data, before large amounts of unstructured data began to be collected.

Unstructured data is not necessarily amenable for storage in a database and is often stored in a graph database. Companies use content management systems, known in the business as CMSs to store unstructured data. Although CMSs are not formally structured like a relational database, they can be searched in real time.

Chapter 4: Predictive Analytics

In this chapter, we will investigate an area of data analysis called predictive analytics. More than fifty years ago, we learned about predictive analytics from Hollywood and the science fiction author Arthur C. Clarke in the story *2001: A Space Odyssey*. In the movie, everything appears to be running fine, but the artificially intelligent computer detects a pending failure in a communications unit. The computer even tells us when the unit will fail. When the unit is removed and studied, the astronauts discover it is not defective, calling into question the previously unquestioned capabilities of the computer.

That part is not relevant for our discussion, but the point of this story is that it had the basic concept of predictive analytics in mind. That is, trying to anticipate and/or prevent some future event based on data regarding a device, customer, or patient.

Predictive analytics is anticipated to have applications in many areas, and as the field is developed, interest by large corporations, sporting organizations, manufacturers, and governments are sure to be high. We will explain what predictive analytics is, who uses it, how it is used, and how it is tied to big data.

What Is Predictive Analytics?

The purpose of predictive analytics is to make predictions about future events, which can have wide applications. For example, the manufacturer of an aircraft might want to predict an engine failure. On the other hand, a service like Netflix might want to predict when a subscriber will cancel their service.

If you run a hedge fund or large stock brokerage, you might be interested in learning what signs occur in market data just before a bear market crash. Medical professionals studying cardiovascular disease could be interested in determining if changes occur in certain blood markers when a heart attack is imminent. Another example could be used in the financial world. Credit card or loan companies might look for behavior patterns that occur just before a person will default on a loan.

In each case, the problems seem very different at first glance, but they have a lot in common—looking for certain patterns in the data that will be a precursor to the event they wish to analyze. For example, on Netflix, you might find certain changes to watching patterns. Maybe the frequency with which the app is opened decreases below a certain threshold. Or users may still open the app, but they may spend more time browsing rather than selecting shows or movies to watch.

With predictive analytics, you will be looking for certain factors to come together to indicate that such an event is about to occur. Before doing any analysis, we might not know what those factors are. In the discussion about Netflix, we are merely speculating. That kind of guesswork is not the kind of information that companies are after today, so they need to use big data to get the answers.

To determine what factors need to come together for the event we want to predict, large amounts of data should be collected and analyzed. The benefit is that you will find many past failures. Continuing to use Netflix as an example, they have tens of millions of subscribers, so there is ample data to analyze the behavior of people who canceled their subscriptions.

Why Use Predictive Analytics?

The purpose of using predictive analytics is so that companies can adopt a proactive stance. That is, they need to take action before the event happens. There is nothing magical going on here. When the company can proactively deal with the situation, then it can intervene before the failure or service cancellation occurs.

In the case of the airplane engine, the plane can be grounded and send for an inspection. The patterns that might emerge when studying past engine failures might provide the information necessary to enact appropriate repairs. An engine failure won't happen unexpectedly, even if before doing your analysis you do not know what systems within the engine tend to fail. This information may be learned using the tools of predictive analytics. With this information in hand, the company can enact repairs on those systems to significantly lower the probability of engine failure.

In the case of behavior that predicts default on a loan, the company could contact the customer to make new payment arrangements to avoid the default. The Netflix example is very common today. Netflix will be very interested in determining if someone is likely to consider canceling their subscription. If they can get this information, then they can take action to try to keep the subscriber. They can start presenting the customer with renewal offers that propose a discount if they renew their subscription within a limited time period. This proactive stance would help the company avoid losing large numbers of users.

The Role of Statistics

The science fiction example we began the chapter with had important information in it. This type of approach in real life won't be considered a success or failure when applied to a sample size of one. Continuing with the Netflix example, we obviously can't deem the data correct if one subscriber predicted to cancel doesn't do so, or if another that didn't meet the criteria ends up canceling. This is a phenomenon rooted in statistics. It will give probabilities and will only have meaning when applied to large numbers of cases, possibly on the order of tens of thousands or more. The more people you apply this to, the more accurate the prediction will be.

The best we could hope for is something akin to the following. Maybe Netflix identifies five behaviors that tend to come together when a subscriber will cancel within thirty days. However, it is not an absolute rule. It might tell you that there is a 90 percent chance the subscriber will cancel, and perhaps subscribers who showed four, or fewer, or even none of the behaviors would cancel. Maybe if the subscriber only exhibits four of the behaviors, there is a 75 percent chance of cancellation. If they show none of the behaviors, there could be a 15 percent chance of cancellation. These examples illustrate how predictive analytics could be applied in practice to avert an undesirable event.

How to Generate Predictions

So far, we have discussed how predictive analytics could be used once the information is known. Now let us consider how we go about getting that information in the first place.

We must start with a source of data. Predictive analytics works best with structured data, but it can work with unstructured data as well. To provide accurate predictions, large amounts of data are required. In statistics, we know that the more data you collect, the more accurate your relationships will. If you are not an expert in statistics, you can see this when polls are taken for political elections. Any poll that does not report the amount of error should be immediately ignored, but most of them will tell you that the results could vary by +/- 3 percent or something to this effect. A poll that showed candidate A was leading candidate B by 49 percent–47 percent, with a margin of error of +/- 3 percent, would be completely worthless. This is because the data could be wrong, and the real result could shift up by 3 percent or down by 3 percent in a variety of ways. To be significant, the difference between the candidates would have to be larger than the error. If the same poll had instead found A to be leading B by a margin of 52 percent to 47 percent, we could take those results more seriously. The other result would indicate that the race was tied.

Something else you will notice about political polls is the larger the sample size, the more accurate the poll results. This is because the margin of error and the sample size are inversely related. You can consult your favorite statistics book to see the specific mathematical formulas if you are interested in the details.

The point is that we need big data. Companies have the data on hand, but they won't be willing to take action based on information that has a large amount of error in today's environment.

Enter Machine Learning

We cover more details about machine learning in a later chapter, but it could play a leading role in predictive analytics. Machine learning can help us find patterns and relationships in any big data we already have. With predictive analytics, this is exactly what we need. For example, Netflix collects information about its subscribers every time you use—and even do not use—Netflix on your television or other devices. This not only includes how often you open the application but what you do once you open it. It tracks what you watch and records other behaviors as well, such as whether the user immediately opens a popular Netflix program or searches for an older movie or TV program. Nearly a million questions could be asked, and Netflix probably has all the answers within their reams of data.

This is a classic big data problem. Not all the data collected from tens of millions of people will be something engineers can look at in a spreadsheet and provide the answers management is seeking. It will require computer power to analyze it.

Machine learning can be used to train a computer system. For example, Netflix would feed a computer data on the viewing habits of people who have already canceled their subscriptions. Then the computer would be unleashed to evaluate the data to discover hidden patterns, trends, and relationships between different behaviors or factors not immediately obvious to human eyes.

Before the data is analyzed, we could not possibly know what the factors are. Once machine learning has been used to train the computer system to find out what they are, then the computer can be used to analyze data coming in from existing users. From here, it can flag users who meet the criteria. This will allow Netflix to take action to try to prevent the subscriber from canceling.

Product Improvement

Predictive analytics also has other advantages. Such an analysis might reveal how a product or service could be improved. Rather than waiting for someone to get to the point of canceling their subscription, Netflix might see what factors are causing people to cancel and then make changes to their service to better meet customer demands.

This approach can be used in any situation. Consider the previous example of an engine failure on an aircraft. Over the short term, the factors that precede engine failure could be used to ground a plane and bring it in for an inspection and possible repairs. Over the long term, the design of the engine could be modified. The modification would proceed based on the new knowledge of what system failures were occurring prior to an actual engine failure. More robust systems could be designed, or specific components could be redesigned to increase the reliability of the system as a whole.

Benefits of Predictive Analytics

Predictive analytics won't create completely flawless systems. However, before predictive analytics and big data, companies had to act based on very limited information and relied on educated guesses and hunches. As a result, the efficiency in operations, reliability in products, and quality of services were not nearly as good as it could be.

Although predictive analytics cannot provide you with 100 percent reliability (nothing can do that anyway), it takes guessing out of the process. Over time, predictive analytics can also be refined. If a company can predict failure to a 90 percent probability, in a few years, they may be able to push that to 95 percent or higher. The more data the company can collect, the more the predictive analytical tools can be refined and improved.

The result is that there will be many benefits both to the company and to the people they serve. First, companies that manufacture products can build products that are safer, more reliable, and offer better performance, overall. Those that offer services can improve them to better meet the needs of their customer base.

Suppose Netflix found that customers who are likely to cancel skip the screen showing current, popular Netflix programs and instead immediately search for movies shown in theaters. Netflix could improve its service by identifying which behavior a user is more likely to engage in. They could then personalize the startup screen seen by each user to better meet their needs.

The Process of Predictive Analytics

The predictive analytics process will move through many stages. Like any activity within a large organization, it will begin by defining the problem. The problem must be defined precisely so that models and computer systems have something specific to tackle, and all members of the organization understand the goals. The scope of the effort should be more limited to get more reliable results.

Once the problem has been identified, big data comes in. This is where the role of the data scientist becomes more important. Data scientists in the organization must determine the best data sources to tackle and solve the problem.

Data has often already been collected, but, if necessary, there can be a data collection stage. In some cases, the need for certain data may be identified in the planning stage. While this will cause some delays in moving forward, if the data is required for a solution to the problem, this step will be essential.

Once the data sets are selected or become available, the data science team can begin a preliminary analysis. This will include the framing of hypotheses and preliminary modeling. Various algorithms are available to use with machine learning that we will go over later in the book. For now, just be aware that the data science team would analyze the data to determine which algorithms are most suitable to get the results they are seeking.

Next, the test data will be selected, and the type selected will depend on many factors. For example, you will have some known data in some cases. This could be the case for a subscription service like Netflix. Certainly, the company would have information that would include subscribers who have canceled their service. The company may even have survey data from a subset of users. Some companies may attempt to ask users some simple questions to get at the reasons for cancellation. A preliminary examination of the data may also reveal some inputs that correlate to the output at hand, which is canceling the service. However, that data may not be available, but it does not matter because machine learning can proceed either way.

The next step is to train the system on subsets of data. This is the learning phase of machine learning. The system will be presented with data, and it will seek out patterns, correlations, and trends that can be used for future estimates.

At each step, the data science team will analyze the results, and the learning process can continue until the team is satisfied with the current state of performance.

At this point, the models can be deployed in real time. Netflix models can be used to read data from customers as it's coming in, and they predict future cancellations. As mentioned earlier, the company will probably aim to predict cancellation behavior several weeks ahead of time to give them time to adjust for the consumer and keep them from going ahead with the cancellation.

Prescriptive Analytics

As the model is in operation, the results will be evaluated on a continual basis to look for areas of improvement. A process called prescriptive analytics can be used to analyze the performance of the model and update it if necessary to improve performance. It can also be used to respond to changing conditions in real time. Keep in mind that changes are always happening in today's fast-paced world.

Applications of Predictive Analytics

As we have shown, businesses and other large organizations can use predictive analytics in many ways. Some of the applications can be quite surprising, but applications of big data usually are. Let us familiarize ourselves with some general applications of predictive analytics.

Healthcare

The function of predictive analytics in healthcare are quite numerous. One common problem that occurs in hospitals is secondary infections. Patients might come in with a viral or other illness and then contract bacterial pneumonia while in the hospital. This problem is ripe for machine learning, provided that the data is available. Big data could be used in conjunction with machine learning to develop models that would estimate a patient's risk for developing secondary infections. The hospital could take steps to reduce the risk, such as keeping patient exposure to others at a minimum during their hospital stay. Nursing and other healthcare staff could also implement extra protection and handwashing measures.

Another application in the healthcare arena is determining who is at risk for different diseases before symptoms occur. For example, patients could be analyzed to determine their risk of developing diabetes or heart disease. Big data analytics could be used to find patterns in the data for breast and prostate cancer, identifying patients that are at high risk of developing these diseases using previously unknown hidden patterns so that intervention or additional screening could be applied.

Both big data and predictive analytics can be used to improve staffing in hospitals. For example, we could determine the best times or days to increase staffing using predictive analytics and determine where to allocate that staffing.

Customer Relations

We have already discussed the issue of customer relations by closely examining how a subscription service like Netflix could improve service and retain customers. Predictive analytics could be used in many other ways for customer relations. For example, using data from previous customer calls, predictive analytics can predict when a customer is about to become irate and cause difficulties for customer service personnel. A series of steps could then be developed to diffuse the situation and help the customer feel they are receiving good customer service.

Sales and Marketing

The application of predictive analytics to sales, advertising, and marketing is huge, and you are probably experiencing that every time that you get on the computer. It can be applied in many ways. If you recall, we mentioned the concept of a Facebook lookalike audience, which is essentially an example of using machine learning, big data, and predictive analytics together. The system, in this case, is examining the various characteristics of Facebook users and using them to predict which customers will purchase a given product.

Predictive analytics can also be used for cross-selling and upselling customers. Big data can be collected on customers who did or did not respond to the cross-selling of a related product. Then it can be analyzed using the techniques of machine learning to find the trends, patterns, and correlations hidden in the data. Once these are known, they can predict which customers are likely to respond.

You can even take this a step further, using split testing of different marketing and advertising methods, down to variations in copy to generate large data sets that can be analyzed. The system can then predict which customers will respond to which message or type of marketing. This will allow a company to develop more personalized and tailored marketing campaigns. They are likely to be far more effective and please the customer more as well, since they will be getting more of what they want rather than being bombarded with irrelevant advertising.

Fraud Detection

Fraud detection is one of the biggest areas in big data, and there are many ways it can be applied. One popular application of predictive analytics is looking for characteristics of tax returns, loan applications, and other financial data that indicate identity theft or some other type of fraudulent activity. Banks use predictive analytics to detect suspicious behavior that could indicate a debit card has been lost or stolen. Like anything else, these detection methods do not always work with complete accuracy, but the more data that is collected, the more accurate they become, reducing the number of false positives. More importantly, predictive analytics can catch cases of stolen cards, put a stop to the transactions, and refund the customer. Fraud detection can also be applied to phony insurance claims.

Credit Approval

One of the most popular ways predictive analytics has been used in recent years is in credit approval for loan applications. Big data has made much information available about people applying for credit over many years. This data has revealed hidden patterns and correlations used in predictive analytics. The patterns in the data have revealed previously unknown correlations that go beyond the simple calculation of a credit score to completely analyze an applicant to determine their risk of default on a loan. The data can also determine other risk factors that could prevent the loan from being paid off, such as the risk of bankruptcy, future unemployment, and even major illnesses that could result in the customer being unable to pay their bills. What is stunning about this trend is that it enables companies to determine the real risk of a given customer defaulting on their loan within seconds. There are downsides to this. There may be cases when a person-to-person interaction might help someone who has risk factors, as their circumstances may have changed. The automatic systems only go with probabilities and what the data says that instant, so they will probably err at times. Overall, the predictive analytics used in this type of application has proven to be extremely accurate.

Military Applications

The Pentagon is using predictive analytics to improve the efficiency of military forces, and, no doubt, other countries are using it as well. It can be used to determine the best way to allocate force deployments based on incoming data, for example, naval vessels could be moved from one location to another. It would also be useful in improving the efficiency of logistics, and stop fuel wasting, reduce idle time, and eliminate other problems the military might encounter.

Law Enforcement and Fire and Rescue

We have already touched on some of the applications of big data to law enforcement. Predicting where and when future crimes will occur is where predictive analytics is married with big data to help law enforcement in a more efficient way. This can occur on several levels. For example, past data will indicate where and when most crimes occur. The variation in crime patterns and types of crime might change with time of year, or based on a myriad of other factors we may not be able to determine ahead of time. By predicting when and where various crimes are more likely to occur, the deployment of police in the field can be made more efficient. This can even be taken down to the level of specific crimes. For example, it might be known that on certain days of the week or months of the year, there are more auto thefts in one part of a city, while there are more rapes and assaults in another. This can help law enforcement not only allocate resources to various locations, but it can also help them determine what types of resources to move to what locations and when they should do it.

Predictive analytics can also be used in larger applications such as drug trafficking. Big data collected on previous movements of drug traffickers, including arrests, can be used to better allocate different types of resources. In some cases, more effort might be required at certain airports, while other resources may be applied to different border areas. The data can be updated in real time to continually adjust the models, as drug traffickers adjust their strategies in response to changing enforcement.

These same methods can be used for the deployment of fire and rescue, and even for deployment locations and levels of Coast Guard resources to get the most efficiency possible. In these cases, predictive analytics can be developed by looking at past data that could indicate where and when most auto accidents occur. Other information can be gleaned, such as the frequency of heart attacks in different areas and at different times. This can help officials put forward more efficient staffing, locate fire stations in the best places, and deploy and adjust resources as necessary.

Regarding the Coast Guard, a similar approach could be used. Fishing vessels often need rescue efforts. Using past data collected on rescue operations, the Coast Guard could predict where accidents are most likely to occur at a given time, and resources could be pre-positioned to improve the efficiency and speed of response.

Other Applications

There are endless applications of predictive analytics. A football team could use data on games played in certain conditions to make predictions about the outcome of various types of strategies, or even players used in the game to determine the best possible outcome.

One problem that has been a constant for business is knowing the best price to charge for a product. In the past, companies had to rely on trial and error to find the sweet spot that maximizes profits while getting the most sales possible. Now that is not the case. Instead of guessing and then seeing what happens, companies can use predictive analytics to determine ahead of time what the best pricing point will be. Keep in mind that these predictions are not set in stone; more data can always be collected, and then the price could be adjusted as necessary.

Another area where this can be utilized is with sales pitches. The results of different approaches can be used to collect data on closing large ticket sales to help improve performance. This is helpful both to the sales staff and to prospective customers. Predictive analytics can tease out specific behaviors that indicate a customer won't ever buy, for example. Sales staff can be trained to recognize these signs, and they can then allocate their efforts more efficiently. This would be done by backing off from customers who are not interested and redirecting efforts to customers most likely to close a sale.

The big advantage of predictive analytics is that it eliminates the guesswork. Having to guess or use hunches at critical points in company operations has always been a weak spot, but now that weak spot is being eliminated.

It appears at first glance that this only helps large corporations, but that is not true. As you probably know, data is for sale everywhere. This means small businesses can leverage data that has been collected by large firms to improve their operations and prospects as well.

Chapter 5: Internet of Things (IoT)

The Internet of Things is a simple concept to understand, but a very powerful concept to implement. When people speak of the Internet of Things, they are referring to any device that can be assigned an IP address and connected to the internet. Technology included in the device can transmit data over the internet. In addition, the device could receive data from the internet and be identified by a unique IP address.

The Internet of Things spans a wide variety of potential technologies. This includes security cameras, doorbells, refrigerators, televisions, wearables, and sensors placed on vehicles. You may be observing that your smartphone, and possibly iWatch or another device, is connected to the internet. While this fits in with the idea of the Internet of Things, the idea is to add internet connectivity to ordinary objects.

The Smart Home

The so-called smart home was one of the earliest ideas that quantified what Internet of Things would mean. A smart home would have all its devices and appliances connected to the internet. This could have practical applications, such as allowing the resident of the home to turn on lights and heat or air conditioning before returning home.

Some aspects of the smart home are limited to practicality. Apple includes a software library called the HomeKit, which allows developers to create software for the iPhone that would allow the user to control various home appliances while either on-site or remotely. These types of systems could also be integrated with Siri or Amazon Alexa to allow voice commands to control various devices.

Using CO_2 sensors, office buildings and homes could be made more efficient by automatically turning on lights and heating/cooling systems when a given room is occupied, while automatically turning off devices when the room is not occupied.

Energy efficiency is one hoped for application of the Internet of Things. Some utility companies have been installing "smart meters" that can be used for two-way communication, not only providing the energy company with information about energy use in the home but possibly even allowing the energy company to set energy usage allowed in the home. Already, many utility companies throughout the country have installed systems that allow them to monitor electricity and gas usage without having to send someone on the property to check it directly.

Ring Doorbells and Security Systems

Home security systems have traditionally used phone lines to connect with security companies and/or police. Recently, however, these companies are looking to take advantage of the internet for security purposes. An internet-connected security system can send information out via the internet if a window is broken or there is a forced entry through a doorway. In addition, residents can purchase home security cameras that can be connected to the internet to monitor the property when they are away from home.

The ring doorbell system is a doorbell with a camera system connected to the internet. This enables the resident to view people coming to the home even when the home occupant is at a different location. Some people have raised privacy concerns, as police are reportedly tapping into the ring doorbell system to monitor neighborhoods.

Transportation

Vehicles can be connected to the internet. For example, a device on the car can monitor speed and driving habits and transmit this information to the insurance company for analysis. Other applications include the automatic collection of tolls and even communication between vehicles on the road to reduce the probability of an accident. Similar technology could be used with self-driving cars. The company can also monitor transportation fleets used by companies remotely. This can be used to develop more efficient ways to operate, potentially saving large amounts of money.

Wearable Technology

Wearable technology has started catching on, first with simple devices like the Fitbit, and more recently with more sophisticated and comprehensive technology like the Apple Watch. Such devices can be easily connected to the internet. Some people envision using these devices as real-time health monitors that could contact emergency services if a major health problem is detected.

Health Monitoring

Some health monitoring will take place via wearable technology; however, some have proposed a "smart toilet" that could analyze waste products and determine whether they represent a possible health problem, and then contact the doctor. For example, blood could be detected in urine or feces, possibly indicating a urinary tract infection, kidney problem, or, in the latter case, colon cancer or a bleeding ulcer.

Big Data and the Internet of Things

These are just a few examples of the many devices that could be used in the Internet of Things. There is no question that with everything from smart homes to wearable technology, huge amounts of data will be generated. Already, even though many of these technologies have not been widely adopted, it is estimated that 4.4 trillion GB of data is generated per year by IoT.

To analyze all this data, big data must be called in. This data will be streamed in real time as sensors found in people's homes, on their bodies, or in the infrastructure of the cities in which they live collects and sends real-time data. This will be a complex problem to deal with because the amounts of data are staggering.

The data generated by the Internet of Things will be unstructured data and received by the companies and sent for data processing. How the data is processed will be influenced by the velocity, variety, and volume. Tools used to store and analyze such data include Hadoop MapReduce and Spark.

The biggest challenge with big data and the Internet of Things is the latency problem. The data will be streaming in real time, and it will require very fast analytics to process. Many experts believe that available technology will be stretched thin by the massive amounts of data collected in real time using the Internet of Things.

The way the data is processed will be familiar. It will be analyzed to spot hidden patterns and trends in the data, along with correlations not obvious to human observers. Companies can use this information to provide customers with better products and services that meet their needs in a more efficient manner.

One way it is hoped the Internet of Things will benefit customers and businesses alike is with the capacity to receive real-time data on the performance of consumer devices, whether it's an automobile, refrigerator, or washing machine. By collecting huge amounts of real-time data from devices as they are being used, companies will be more able to predict coming faults, and they will also be able to build more reliable devices in the future. Being able to detect problems earlier will also help companies deliver better customer service. It is also expected that, to a certain degree, having internet-connected devices will enable them to repair themselves, at least in certain situations.

Big data combined with the Internet of Things is likely to revolutionize the healthcare industry. It will enable healthcare providers to provide remote diagnosis capabilities. In addition, there can be improved patient monitoring in real time, allowing doctors to spot problems earlier and even possibly delivering medications remotely.

Companies that have delivery fleets like UPS can use the Internet of Things to closely monitor the use of their vehicles. This will help them identify points where efficiency can be increased, while closely monitoring driver behavior. Waste can be significantly reduced, and each driver can be monitored for driving habits, for example, noting if they speed or drive roughly in ways that would be detrimental to the vehicle.

Elder Care

It is expected that the Internet of Things can play a large role in improving the care of the elderly, often allowing more elderly people to remain living independently in their own homes for longer periods. This can include assistance with managing the house such as lighting and heat/cooling systems. Also, the elderly will be able to be tracked for health problems with devices that can detect medical issues as they arise.

Privacy Issues

The Internet of Things is not a concept without controversy. Many people are concerned with privacy issues. If data is being constantly streamed from your home, it has the potential of being hacked. Some people are even worried about companies and even governments abusing systems like this, with the ability to reach into the home and make changes to appliances or adjust the thermostat. The potential for hacking also looms large with cameras. It remains to be seen whether the Internet of Things will be accepted by the general public. The recent explosion in concern over privacy issues related to social media companies has put this into doubt to a certain extent. Even the ring doorbell has generated a lot of controversy, even though it seems like a basic and common-sense idea.

Many people are beginning to be put off regarding the idea that they will be monitored all the time. Already, people are getting uncomfortable simply being tracked while they are browsing the internet. If your refrigerator can be monitored too, then this is sure to generate much controversy among the public, and it is not clear that people will eagerly adopt such new technologies.

At the time of writing, politicians in the United States and Europe are falling all over themselves talking about regulating the big technology companies. It is unclear where all this talk will lead. Some politicians think they can solve the privacy issues by breaking up the big tech companies. However, this is certainly not going to stop the development of these kinds of technologies, and it might even make privacy issues worse since the information will not be controlled and analyzed by the big companies but might find its way into multiple hands.

Chapter 6: Data Mining

When confronted with large data sets, it is important to get relevant information from the data. This process goes by the name *data mining* in some contexts. Data mining is the process of examining big data to find the patterns it contains. There are many aspects involved in data mining, including regression analysis, detecting anomalies in the data, using machine learning, and clustering. We will examine these factors in this chapter and explore the concept of data mining.

Data mining can be applied to almost any industry. Some industries where it has already been used extensively include banking and finance, personally tailored marketing, detection of spam email, and fraud detection in general.

Raw data is often highly disorganized. To utilize it, an organization must have staff on hand that can access the data, do some preliminary analysis, and organize it in useful and productive ways. There are several weak points in the process of data mining, but they are easy to manage effectively with a little planning. Although artificial intelligence and machine learning, along with raw computational power in general, will play a large role in data mining, the human element remains a crucial part of the process.

Data Mining: What Is It?

Data mining is just another way to describe the process of finding hidden patterns that exist in large data sets. Multiple methods can be utilized to discover these patterns. These include using the methods of statistics and tools like regression to help researchers build a relationship between input and output data. Machine learning often plays a central role in the process of data mining because machine learning is often far more effective than human analysis regarding extracting hidden patterns within data sets.

Several core elements must be in place to use data mining. The first of these is either an effective method of data collection or the ability to obtain data from third-party sources. Second, you must have warehousing in place, which essentially involves the ability to store all this data. Cloud computing has made this capacity accessible even to small businesses. Next, it is important to have the required computer processing power. These form the core components that can then be used in conjunction with machine learning algorithms to produce models for predicting future outcomes.

The main point regarding data mining is that it grew out of efforts to find patterns in data without using any hypothesis of what those patterns might be beforehand. The purpose of data mining is the same purpose that lies behind many, if not most, uses of big data. That is, you want to use data mining to make future predictions. For businesses, this can help them retain customers, improve service, cut operational costs, increase product reliability and safety, and more.

Data mining was originally used with databases, so is most closely associated with structured data. It was one of the first efforts that grew out of modern computer technology calling upon interdisciplinary skills. These include computer science, using artificial intelligence and machine learning, along with statistics and probability. As computing power has increased over the years and costs have declined, the ability to use data mining has increased and expanded.

In the past, researchers had to do much manual work, developing models that would essentially be educated guesses, and then writing software to go through the data and do the work. However, machine learning has changed this process. Now manual work has been minimized, restricted to choosing the type of model to use and selecting data sets that can be incorporated in training the artificially intelligent system. Then the computer can do all the work, learning from the data and rapidly finding hidden connections and patterns that were previously unknown to the business or organization.

While early data mining efforts were focused on structured data, things have changed a lot in the past twenty-five years. Unstructured data now makes up an estimated 90 percent of all data collected. With unstructured data, there is more potential for discovering hidden information, so this data can be extremely useful.

However, unstructured data also presents many important problems. From the point of view of a human observer, this data is noisy. This is why machine learning can play a large role in modern data mining efforts. Machine learning makes it possible to sift through the apparent noise and chaos and do it in a relatively fast period. This allows organizations of various types to gather important information from their data, including previously hidden correlations and trends. Data mining is used in conjunction with predictive analytics to develop effective predictive models that can be enforced to future data to predict possible outcomes.

Data Mining Software

Many software tools are specifically designed for data mining purposes. The software can be used to classify data and group it into useful clusters for future analysis. This will be used in conjunction with data warehousing, which is the process of storing and analyzing the data. Usually, the data is collected from multiple sources. Data warehouses can run queries on the data as well as do analysis, but one of the main functions of data warehousing is to store the data electronically so they can be accessed. This process can involve consolidating data from different sources and using analysis to extract relevant data that can be used for predictive analytics and other purposes. Data mining is the process of looking for patterns in the data.

Descriptive Modeling

Several techniques used in data mining fall under the umbrella of descriptive modeling. The goal of descriptive modeling is to use past data that has been collected to uncover factors that played a role in the failure or success of products, services, and activities. Several techniques are utilized in descriptive modeling to improve future outcomes by producing more products that are reliable and help to improve the match of company services to customer desires.

Clustering

The first technique we will examine in this process is called clustering, which forms "clusters" of objects or data points that share certain characteristics. For example, in a customer database, you might develop clusters of customers by gender and age. One cluster might be females aged thirty-five to forty. Clusters are used with data mining to develop an exploratory process that might find important correlations in the data. Statistics play an important role in developing the appropriate clusters. The idea is to get a group of data that has more similarities than differences as compared to other clusters.

The type of data does not have to be structured or related to people, so the example above is just one such example. Clustering could be used in image analysis or other applications where the data is unstructured and impersonal. When building clusters, scientists use a distance function defined for the specific problem at hand. The concept will be an abstract one for most applications, but it is mathematically similar to the standard distance functions used in algebra and basic physics. It turns out that "distance" is a general concept, and if you have the right data points to examine, you can determine an abstract distance not based on physical location but based on characteristics and properties that can help you find similar or different data points. To use it properly, a distance threshold would have to be defined to determine the membership in one cluster or another for a specific data point.

One way this could be used is in grouping pixels together to form an image. Rather than grouping them by their location in the image, you might group them by color instead. For example, you can set a threshold to determine whether a pixel qualifies as "red," "green," "blue" etc., and then in your data analysis, you would group them in this fashion, again ignoring other properties like image location. An alternative examination could develop different clusters of the data. You could look at the brightness of each cluster instead, and group pixels according to different levels of brightness.

Anomaly Detection

Anomaly detection looks for data points that are outliers. The definition of an outlier must be precisely defined, but anomaly detection is a very important tool used in data mining because outliers often represent important problems. There is always noise in the data, so errors must be quantified. One obvious application of anomaly detection is using medical scans such as a CT scan or MRI, that might discover differences in tissue density and so forth that could be caused by the presence of a tumor or foreign object.

Anomaly detection is also important for detecting fraud. When there are data points that are outliers, this is often a strong indication that something is awry. Anomalies can take many forms. It might take the form of data far outside the norm. However, it could also take the form of an unusual frequency of data. Often, when people are trying to break into computer networks, this could result in a spike in access attempts.

Anomaly detection can be used to detect spam emails. This can be based on the method of contact or the content of the message. For example, emails that demand payment or that ask the user to reveal certain important personal information can be flagged as anomalies.

Machine learning can play a central role in anomaly detection. It can be trained one of two ways, which will be discussed in more detail later. One way machine learning can be trained is to provide the system with input and output data from past experiences that are thoroughly known. For example, the computer system can be fed information related to bank fraud, which could include inputs of various types together with outputs that indicate either normal transactions or fraudulent transactions. By studying the inputs and outputs, the machine can learn how to appropriately tune various parameters to accurately predict the outcomes of future events.

Sometimes that type of data is not known, or we want the computer to find hidden anomalies. Large data sets can be passed into the system. Presumably, most data collected is "normal." Most banking data, for example, will involve perfectly normal and legal transactions that do not involve any kind of fraud. Maybe one case out of a thousand is fraudulent. You let the system work on large data sets to learn what is normal and what is not.

Typical applications of anomaly detection include network intrusion or hacking attempts, spam email, insurance fraud, loan application and bank fraud, tax fraud, and unusual activity detected with sensor networks. Anomaly detection is also used for data security, with mixed results so far.

Many techniques are used in fraud detection. First off, remember that this kind of work will be probability-based. Therefore, the techniques of statistics are often brought to the problem. In some cases, fraud will be missed, and in others, there will be false positives. Bayesian networks can help maximize the probability of success. Clustering can also be used since grouping data points will reveal outliers that are classified according to a certain distance level. Nearest neighbor techniques are also useful in detecting outlying data points.

Association Rules

Another task performed during data mining is to look for hidden relationships between the data. There are many applications of this. For example, you might analyze data of women aged thirty-five to forty to see what drinks they order with what types of food in restaurants. Or you might determine what shoes they purchase on Amazon while purchasing clothing items. All kinds of associations may exist in data.

Classification

The classification problem generally involves sorting data into bins. The simplest classification problem will be one that is binary in nature. You could analyze customers of your cell phone network and classify whether they are Android or iOS users. One of the most famous classification problems is that of detecting spam email. By searching for characteristics and text snippets that are commonly used in spam email, the system can use an either-or method to classify an email as spam or not. In the real world, this must be done on a threshold basis. An email might show 45 percent of the known characteristics of a spam message. In that case, it would be classified as not spam if the threshold were set to 50 percent. A message with 55 percent would definitely be classified as spam. However, these types of detection methods are obviously not perfect, which is why even though it has gotten better over the years, email systems still commit frequent errors with this task.

Regression

Regression is a technique that attempts to get data into an input-output relationship of the form $y = f(x)$. Given inputs x, which could be a vector, you get outputs y. By examining large amounts of data, a computer system can fit the data to an equation or sets of equations to make predictions when presented with future input data. If the data set is suitable for this type of analysis, the training will probably involve what is called labeled data. The labeling is that the data is labeled as input or output, and the computer is exposed to known answers so it can start learning the parameters involved in the relationship. These are tuned and then if the data set is large enough, they are likely to be highly accurate.

In the past, people had to make educated guesses with parameters in the equations, and repeatedly test and adjust until they arrived at the right answer through manual work. Now, this can be done with real-time adjustments made by the computer system itself with the machine learning process.

Knowledge Discovery in Databases (KDD)

This is a staged way to go about finding patterns in data. Data mining is part of this process, but it is not the only aspect of KDD. The process begins with selecting the appropriate data. Humans working on the problem usually do this. It is a very important step; if the wrong data is selected, then you are getting off on the wrong foot.

The data must then go through a stage of pre-processing. This necessary step must be performed for data mining algorithms to work correctly and will involve some judgment. Researchers may have access to very large data sets, or, in some cases, they may not have large amounts of data. Either way, this would be problematic. Although, strictly speaking, more data will produce more accurate results, too much data can mean excessive amounts of time will be required to analyze it and get answers in a timely fashion. Think back to the example of the U.S. Census and how without the invention of the data processing machine, it would have taken nine years to process the data. Certain limits are determined by the current level of technology and the data set. In each application, the organization will have its own time constraints that must be met for the work to be useful. For that reason, sometimes data sets must be trimmed or only subsets of all the available data can be used.

If there is not enough data, then it might not be possible for the system to detect hidden patterns that exist. Another way to say this is that the data would not be statistically significant. In that case, it would be possible, perhaps just as likely, that the system would detect false patterns that do not exist in the data. On the other hand, it will miss existing patterns entirely. We see that determining whether there is enough data will be a part of the pre-processing step.

Data mining is then used to analyze the data. The process may run through several steps. After data mining has been completed, the data science team must interpret and analyze the results to determine whether it is up to the desired level of accuracy. If it is not, then the process can be repeated as necessary. Further trials of learning on the data can help the system approach the desired levels of accuracy.

Once the model is performing at an acceptable level, it can be deployed in the field for use. Although we are presenting some of the techniques and topics in this book independently, this is done to facilitate learning for the beginner who is new to big data and data science. In reality, none of these techniques, methods, or tools, are used and developed in isolation. For example, data mining will be a part of predictive analytics. Machine learning will help systems train before they are deployed for actual use.

Problems with Data Mining

One problem that can arise with data mining is that the wrong hypothesis was chosen to begin with. This can be an important factor in determining the success or failure of a data-mining operation. Second, it is possible to choose the wrong data sets. At other times, the right hypothesis is paired with the wrong data set. As mentioned above, for the results to have validity, the right size is required. If a data set is too small to produce accurate results, the entire operation will be suspect. If the model ends up being deployed anyway, it could be plagued with erroneous predictions.

All models will have some erroneous predictions because statistics is never an absolute result. That is why we can only specify probabilities of accurate results and not definite outcomes the way you can with a simple algebra problem.

This fact has caused some minor problems with data mining. In some cases, fraud goes undetected. Spam emails often find ways to get through. Despite the best efforts, it is not always possible to detect a hacking attempt until after the fact. These results are a fact of life in data mining and predictive analytics, and the reality is they will always be there. As time goes on and more data is collected, accuracy might increase to a degree.

Remember that the systems we are talking about are dynamic systems. As a result, the desired levels of accuracy may not be possible to attain, or they may only be reached for a short period. Spammers are actively at work every day, and they are not just sending out the typical spam messages that have already been flagged. Spammers are constantly working to defeat detection systems. The same goes for many other activities. Since the system is dynamic, it must be constantly monitored and upgraded.

Privacy Issues

In the past year, privacy issues have been coming to the forefront of activities in big tech. One issue of importance is related to a process known as data aggregation, which involves collecting and pooling data collected from many sources. For example, a company might obtain data from Facebook about users and then pool that with payment processing data to develop a new data set that would be highly valuable and could be exploited for various purposes.

This has raised many legal issues. Privacy advocates are extremely concerned about companies sharing data about consumers with other companies. One area where this has recently come up is the use of mobile applications. Some have been found to be sharing the information they collect about users with large companies like Facebook.

This is a natural outcome, but it is unclear how long it will last. Obviously, when data is the new currency among business—since it allows them to precisely target prospects and customers—companies will be strongly motivated to share their data. It can be a very lucrative way to earn money, which is one reason so many free apps and websites have proven to be highly valuable on Wall Street. People naively look at a company and note that it is not making any money from its activities while ignoring the fact that the company can collect large amounts of data that other companies are more than willing to pay high dollars for.

Data aggregation from multiple sources has drawn the attention of authorities from the European Union, and the United States Congress is also becoming alarmed about the privacy issues that arise from the sharing of such data. This is likely to result in some forms of regulation, which will at least require companies to have firm privacy policies and notify customers of how their data will be used.

One defense of data mining in the past was that specific individuals could not be identified. However, with the advent of big data and all that entails, along with the ability to combine multiple data sets into new aggregate data, it is now possible to identify specific individuals even when protections in one or more of the individual data sets used to form the aggregate are in place. This could mean thorny times ahead as politicians begin sticking their noses into this business.

Common Applications

We have already examined one of the most common applications of data mining, and that is in the detection of spam emails. It can also filter emails. If you have noticed recently, large email providers such as Google have taken it upon themselves to classify emails into different types. The Gmail system has a primary email inbox, a social media inbox, and a business-related inbox. Presumably, by dividing up emails in this fashion, it makes the system more efficient for the user. This way if they are looking for a message from Facebook or Twitter, they can immediately go to the social tab. In addition, the system has set up separate junk email folders where spam messages are sent. This can save users a great deal of time since they can quickly scan spam messages for false flags, rather than having to go through all their messages in a single email box.

Another well-known application of data mining is done by grocery stores. In a clever sleight of hand, they raised prices and then offered buyer loyalty cards that could be used to obtain "discount" prices. This has enabled grocery stores to collect huge amounts of data that can track people's purchases, frequency of store visits, and store locations visited. This can then be used to tailor advertising to customers, perhaps by offering them appropriate coupons or sending personalized advertisements to them in the mail.

Chapter 7: Machine Learning

Machine learning is at the core of almost everything involving big data. By itself, huge amounts of data are not worth anything. The relationships hidden in the data along with patterns and possible trends is where the "gold" is regarding big data. To get at this information, it requires the use of computing power. There are different ways to do this, but letting computer systems learn from the data on their own has proven to be the most effective way to get at the value inside large data sets. First, this is obviously far better than using human analysis, since humans are not good at dealing with enormous data sets. Second, while humans may be clever, we are a slow bunch. Computers can do something in an afternoon that might take a team of human beings a dozen years to complete. Even if you had that much time to wait for your results, the lack of efficiency would be an important issue. Solving the problem the first time probably won't result in the most accurate or the best solution.

Before getting into deep discussions of machine learning, it is good to learn a little about its history. First, how is it classified? Machine learning is considered a subset of artificial intelligence. Simply put, computer systems can learn from data sets by a process. This is done largely in an automatic or autonomous manner. That makes it seem kind of mysterious, but in reality, machine learning is down to earth, and it won't involve roaming androids like in the movie Blade Runner—at least not yet.

Machine learning has been used in a wide variety of applications. It is particularly useful for identifying waste in a complex system. As mentioned earlier, Southwest Airlines and UPS analyze the behaviors of pilots and drivers and look for points where fuel, time, and other resources were being wasted. Machine learning is also playing a central role in the development of self-driving vehicles. Whether full-blown self-driving cars and trucks will ever be on the road, the technologies being developed in the pursuit of this technology will certainly be incorporated into human-operated vehicles to make them safer and more reliable.

Machine learning can tease out patterns that could be applied in law enforcement. It has already been used to help investigators identify terrorists. One possible application the United States should consider is the coalescing of multiple data sets from social media and firearms purchases. They could then look for patterns that might identify potential mass shooters before they carry out the act or post some kind of demented manifesto.

It's important to keep in mind that machine learning should not be viewed as a magic pill, but it will no doubt be used in more and more applications going forward. It is clear that if machine learning does not eliminate your job, it will certainly impact it. The economy will face major disruption in the next two decades as machine learning and artificial intelligence become more mainstream and widely used.

A Brief History of Machine Learning

The first attempt to develop machine learning happened way back in 1957, at IBM, which was then the leading technology company on the planet. A computer scientist named Arthur Samuel developed a software program that used machine learning to play checkers. You are probably aware that over the years, IBM developed better and better supercomputers where we can play chess and could eventually beat human masters at the game. Those developments can be traced back to Samuels' work, which is the first known instance of machine learning. The breakthrough in Samuels' work was that the computer could learn without human intervention and that its skills increased with repetition. That is, the more it played checkers, the better it became at playing the game. Sounds very human, doesn't it? The program could also study and learn which moves would lead to victory.

At about the same time, another engineer named Frank Rosenblatt came up with the idea of a neural network and built the first neural networked computer. A neural network is based on the model of the human brain, which is built out of individual, interconnected neurons. It is important to realize that the "neurons" are software modules, so this is not some kind of artificial cell. By combining this with machine learning, you can create a powerful tool, which is in some sense structured to mimic the activity of a real neural network.

The next step in the development of machine learning didn't happen for another ten years—an algorithm called the nearest neighbor, which is frequently used in today's work. It has proven very important in the science of pattern recognition, which plays a huge role in image processing and pattern recognition in an abstract sense, such as that used with big data.

The 1980s saw huge strides in machine learning. Researchers began teaching computer systems how to create their own rules, and this was used to develop early instances of what we would call robots, which were computer systems in some kind of body that we're able to use machine learning to move through their environment and avoid obstacles.

Since that time, IBM developed the Deep Blue computer, which was able to defeat some of the world's leading chess champions. This was considered an important milestone in the development of machine learning, proving that computer systems could process information and make decisions as well as a human being can, at least under certain conditions. This is a different way of looking at computer systems, since the old idea is computers are good at things humans are slow at, such as adding up a large volume of numbers or going through a spreadsheet to do manual calculations. This event showed that computers could think, again at least in limited applications.

From here, Google, IBM, Facebook, and others have developed more artificially intelligent platforms. Distributed computing has also come on the scene, radically changing the computer resources available to solve different problems.

Early on, the goal among computer scientists was to create a fully autonomous computer system that was artificially intelligent. They were thinking in terms of an "android" as it has been incorporated into science fiction.

The early promises of the computer science community left many people feeling disappointed because they were never realized. Since that time, however, the definition and hopes for artificial intelligence have been tempered somewhat, and now the goal and expectations are that computer systems will be developed that are "smart" in a limited and specialized sense. You won't have independent robots taking over the world, but rather specialized devices performing specific tasks. Machine learning will be playing a larger role going forward because the amount of data being generated will continue to grow at an exponential pace.

What Is Machine Learning?

Machine learning begins by exposing a computer system to sets of data. The idea is that the machine will learn from the data, and so develop on its own for the specific task to which it is being applied. We use the term "machine" in a general sense here, in most cases; this will be a software system. Machine learning is a subfield of artificial intelligence.

What exactly is the machine "learning"? The key to machine learning is that it will use statistical modeling to seek out patterns that are hidden in large data sets. If you are familiar with computer programming, then you know that when you program a computer, many algorithms are used to solve problems. These algorithms have many parameters that should be set to get results from the computer. In the past, programmers may have set the parameters themselves, and then adjusted them after running the program to improve the accuracy of the results.

In the case of machine learning, the parameters are not set. Rather, the system adjusts them as it is exposed to actual data. To a certain degree, the computer operates by learning from the data. Keep in mind that in most applications, this is not some general skill, so it is not like the HAL 9000 computer. We are talking about computer systems learning so that they are good at finding patterns in data related to specific applications.

Training the Machine

With machine learning, before using the system on the real data of interest, it has to be trained just as a small child must go to school and learn the basics of academics. There are two general ways a system is taught. The first method is to use supervised learning.

When you train a system using supervised learning, it will be exposed to data where you know what the answer is. We are providing the system with labeled data. The computer will be provided both the inputs and outputs for the data so it can learn the relationship that exists between them. The data scientist will provide the inputs and outputs but provides no information on what the relationship between these variables is or what it might be. This is for the computer to discover on its own.

Supervised learning has been described as being similar to teaching children in school, perhaps with multiplication tables. The teacher knows the answer to the multiplication tables and guides the children in learning this information.

The goal in machine learning is for the system to learn to seek out patterns between an input variable, and the associated output variable. The hope is that if the computer learns well when it is presented later with inputs where the output variable is unknown, the computer system can provide a good estimate of what the outputs should be. Let us look at this in more detail.

Supervised Learning

Supervised learning involves teaching a computer system about a data set using input and output pairs. Before the work even starts, there is at least a subset of data for which the outputs for a given set of data inputs are known. Sometimes this is referred to as training with labeled data. This terminology is used because the machine is presented with data labeled as input and output. As a very simple example, you could imagine that the probability of default on a loan could be tied to the credit score of the applicant. The input data would be the credit score, while the output data would be the default probability. Thresh-holding could also be used so that if the probability were at a certain level, the applicant would simply be marked as rejected.

Learning is done by presenting the machine or system with pairs of data. In the real world, the input will involve multiple data points. Using the financial example again, this could include age, education level, occupation, income level, and so on. When you store multiple data points into one aggregate piece of data, this is known as a vector. The output does not have to be another vector, but it could be depending on the application at hand.

Supervised learning begins by picking out the appropriate data sets that will be used for training purposes. The training set should be sufficiently general so it can provide the computer with a reasonable representation of the real-world data it will face. This data is then paired with the known outputs that have already occurred to form the training set of data.

Dimensionality is a factor that influences the course of this process. Remember that we have trade-offs to make with big data. The data set must be big enough to find statistically significant patterns in the data. There is a point where a data set can be too big, so much so that it would take a very long time even for modern, distributed, and fast computer systems to analyze.

Likewise, there are trade-offs to be made with data inputs used for training in machine learning and machine learning in general. The number of inputs used to create the input vector is referred to as the dimension of the vector. A vector with five data points—such as the city of residence, income, age, educational attainment, and credit score—would be five-dimensional.

Your first thought might be that the more information you have about a problem, the more accurate your answer will be. Regarding the input vector, that is not the case. Too many variables can make it difficult or impossible to find relationships and patterns in the data. This represents another trade-off—you want enough data points so there is enough information to make accurate predictions, but not too much information that basically overwhelms the system.

Once these issues have been hashed out, the next task is to choose an algorithm. Algorithms commonly used in supervised machine learning include Neural networks, linear regression, logistic regression, Bayesian analysis, decision trees, and nearest-neighbor algorithms. Regression and classification problems are deemed to be well-suited to supervised learning.

The specific choice of the algorithm will be dependent on the judgment of the data science team running the training. This may depend on the nature of the problem at hand, and the team would evaluate the structure and nature of the inputs and outputs and then choose an appropriate algorithm accordingly. Since the outputs are known beforehand, training can proceed until a desired level of accuracy is attained. Then the system can be deployed and used on real data.

Unsupervised Learning

Unsupervised learning proceeds without known outputs. The data, in this case, is considered unlabeled. With unsupervised learning, since the outputs are not known, the main goal of this process is to uncover previously unknown patterns and relationships that may exist in the data. Generally, it is believed that supervised learning produces better training and is more suitable for most tasks. However, unsupervised learning will be useful in cases where the outcomes of previous instances of data inputs are not known.

We have seen possible applications of unsupervised learning before. For example, we talked earlier about clustering. Another use of unsupervised learning is with anomaly detection.

When clustering is used, the goal is to do analysis and try to find algorithmic relationships between clustered data to seek out properties that represent common features among different data points. Clustering can also detect anomalous data. Since clustering involves grouping data points by common features, when a data point appears that cannot fit into any of the known clusters, an anomaly has been recognized.

Some types of neural networks, which are also used with supervised learning, can be used with unsupervised learning as well. The goal here is to use a representation of neural processing in the computer system. When neurons are connecting and firing in response to the presentation of new information, they strengthen the connections between themselves, and this forms a neural network in the brain. The more it is used, the stronger it gets and the better it is at processing data. This is how you learn things and why practice makes perfect.

Similarly, in an artificially intelligent system, you can have nodes that play the role of neurons. As information is presented to the system, various methods are used to strengthen or weaken the connections between nodes and with the input data itself. This is done by using probability levels that can give greater weight or less weight to a given node, or even shut it out completely. The levels of connections are determined by previous exposures of the nodes to the data. The better they learn, the stronger the connections, which enhances learning in the following cycle. Neural networks of this type have been applied to pattern recognition problems. They can identify a person by their face or their fingerprint, for example.

Issues and Trade-offs with Machine Learning

In this section, we will look at some trade-offs that occur regarding machine learning. Remember that everything in life has trade-offs, and some of those trade-offs may be uncomfortable to make. There is no exception regarding machine learning in big data.

We have already touched on some trade-offs that might have to be made. One of the trades is the size of the inputs provided to the system for learning. The more information provided with inputs, the less reliable your results will. A computer system will be a lot better at finding relationships between a given output of say five to seven inputs, as compared to fifty or one hundred inputs. The more you refine the data, the less relevant each new piece of information may be. If we had to determine whether someone is a good credit risk, their current income level might be a relevant piece of data. Their shoe size is probably not relevant. That is an extremely obvious example, but one problem is that, in practice, it might be difficult to decide what is relevant and what is not relevant.

In any case, no matter what the data is, it becomes harder for computers to deal with higher dimensionality regarding the input vector. This will also require a lot more processing time. For those who have a background in probability studies and combinatorics, think about the different ways you can put one object in different number boxes, and then think about all the possible combinations if you keep increasing the number of objects. A computer system could find itself a bit overwhelmed if it has to process too much information, resulting in too many possibilities. The people analyzing the big data will have limited amounts of time within which they need to have a working model, which would put constraints on this process even if the extra data did not lead to mistakes. To solve this problem, it is common for researchers to use dimensionality reduction. Even if a large set of data could be used to create input vectors that had large numbers of properties, it is quite common to cut those down to a smaller level. Just for the sake of an example, suppose we had a dataset with twenty features for each data point to determine whether someone is a credit risk. To whittle the program down to something that can be productive, we might decide to use only five to seven of those features.

One of the most important issues in the process of machine learning is known as the bias-variance trade-off. In the machine learning community, when they talk about bias, they are talking about the error or the average difference between the prediction made by the model and the correct value. This is easy to determine when we are working with supervised learning and have the output values at our disposal. If the bias is high, this means the model has less accuracy. You would prefer a model with lower levels of bias, so it will be more accurate.

Variance is just the term used in statistics, which tells us the spread of the data that the model predicts the actual or correct values. The trade-off results because when machine learning models have high variance, they are well-attuned to the training data, but they cannot generalize the results well and don't work well on new data the model hasn't seen before.

High bias tends to occur when the input model is too small and has too few dimensions or parameters. When a bias is high, variance tends to be low. The opposite situation happens if you have too many parameters. This will lead to high variance but low bias. Data scientists will use their knowledge of statistics to keep the total error in their model at a minimum. The error is determined in part by the bias and the variance.

Remember that any data set will contain some amount of noise. The noise is not relevant to the actual solution to the problem, so if your model is fooled by the noise, it will give inaccurate answers when confronted with new data.

When supervised learning is being used, there are three possibilities. If the data is overfitting, that means it almost exactly matches the actual output. You do not want an exact match, because that means the model is fitting a data set that contains a lot of noise. This is the high variance case—it fits the training data but will not fit new data very well. On the other hand, if the model cannot determine the pattern in the underlying data, it will underfit the data. If it is not able to detect the pattern, you have a high bias. Variance, in that case, will be low, but the model won't be worth very much. You can think of it as generating a straight line that is consistent but does not come close to matching many outputs with any accuracy.

If you minimize the error, then there will be a trade-off of lowering the bias and the variance. The curve generated by the model will fit the pattern of the data closely but will not match it exactly. You accomplish this by having the right number of parameters.

Semi-Supervised Learning

Another way to train for machine learning is called semi-supervised, which can begin by using supervised learning on a small data set. This will wet the feet of the model, so to speak. This is labeled data with inputs and known outputs. After the initial training session on the labeled data, the model is then trained on unlabeled data in an unsupervised training session.

The goal of machine learning is to have a system that can run autonomously. Although there is some human involvement in supervised and semi-supervised learning, once training is completed, the computer will run and make decisions on its own.

Benefits of Machine Learning

The first major benefit regarding machine learning is that it allows you to process large amounts of data, and it is easy to find relationships and patterns that exist. Once they have been identified, these relationships can then be used by the business for productive purposes. Once established and working, a machine-learning model can be repeatedly applied to data mining activities.

This brings us to the second benefit. The original checkers program that launched the machine learning community was able to continue learning every time it played checkers. Moreover, just like when a human learns, the software became better each time it played the game. This means that machine learning gets better with time. The problems a modern business may be seeking to address may be a lot more complex than playing checkers, but once a machine learning system has been trained, it can keep learning and improving its performance and efficiency. As time goes on, the predictions made by the system as it continues to encounter more data will be accurate. Everything hinges on how well the training was done, and the bias-variance trade-off could factor in here.

Machine learning frees up people to do other work. Once trained and deployed, a machine learning system can run entirely on its own. It will continue to learn and adapt, and it can do so without further human intervention. Consider a fraud detection system for a bank. As it encounters more cases of fraud, it will become faster and more accurate when detecting new cases of fraud in the future. Or consider an artificially intelligent anti-virus program. It could adapt to the detection of new viruses as it learns, without the need for further human intervention. This means that when new viruses hit the internet, it will not be necessary for human programmers to write a patch for the anti-viral software.

The ability to put systems like this in place that require little human intervention is a great labor-saving device. People who would normally have to devote massive amounts of attention to things like security are freed up for other tasks.

Another benefit of machine learning is that automation will accelerate. Some people are worried about this, but automation reduces costs, increases productivity, and increases safety. The increase in productivity and efficiency will help boost the economy at large, helping to grow employment and business overall.

Cons of Machine Learning

There are cons associated with every technology, and we would not be honest if we did not talk about the possible cons with machine learning.

The first con is that people have too much faith in machine learning. This means that training could be sloppy, resulting in high bias or high variance. Since people may get overconfident in the ability of the system to learn; they could be deployed too early, resulting in problems with predictability down the road.

Another con is that many resources may have to be expended to get results from machine learning. This will come in the form of money required for computer systems or access, paying data scientists, and time waiting for the system to come online and start delivering the promised results.

Another con is the possibility of "inequality." Having data scientists on staff is expensive, and it may be difficult for small businesses to do. Second, computing time and accessing the right computing power to use machine learning is also very expensive and time-consuming for a small business. The data sources used can cause long time delays in getting a model deployed and operational if they are not chosen wisely. This can create a problem for small businesses that might not be able to afford the extra expenses.

This can put these businesses at a major disadvantage. Large corporations are collecting more and more data, including buying it from other companies, and this is massively improving their efficiency and competitiveness. However, small businesses may simply be unable to compete at this level. This may reduce some of the dynamism in the economy, since it could put small businesses, which used to be the nimble ones, at a competitive disadvantage. Imagine a small company that cannot afford to do machine learning or hire data scientists going up against a larger competitor that has data scientists on staff and access to banks of computers for data mining. The larger company might just run circles around the smaller one.

Another con is the weakness of machine learning systems regarding error. The training process is a vital component of a successful machine learning system. Imagine an error during the training process that is not caught by the data science team. If this happens, since machine-learning systems *learn*, the system will view the error as a fact. This could create a long-term problem that might provide the company with erroneous predictions, but it will be impossible to spot the error. This can create a large waste of time and money as a result. As the system continues to operate, the error will always be there. Since the system is autonomous once it is deployed, this may delay the tracking down of such errors. If the system must be rectified, it will require that the company start from scratch. That means they must start the training program all over again, and hopefully, it will go smoothly the next time around.

Summary

Let us not get too caught up in the potential negatives associated with machine learning. On balance, it is a very powerful and useful tool. Most of the errors and problems associated with it can be avoided by starting off on the right foot and having good data scientists who know what they are doing. The impact of the cons will depend on the specific application. If a company finds that they are getting erroneous results, hopefully, the problems can be identified and rectified quickly.

Chapter 8: Artificial Intelligence

Machine learning is a subfield of artificial intelligence. The goal of artificial intelligence is to create computer systems that work similar to the human mind. As we saw with machine learning, it learns the way a human learns—through experience. In the early days of computer science, engineers and computer scientists explored the notion of artificial intelligence. Even in the 1940s, the idea of the Turing machine, a test developed by the computer scientist Alan Turing, hinted at the possibilities of computers gaining human-like intelligence.

For years, artificial intelligence languished, losing cache after the promises made failed to materialize. However, the problem stemmed from having to wait for computer hardware to catch up to the lofty ideas of artificial intelligence. This has been realized at various points over the past fifty years, as we saw in the last chapter. The development of artificially intelligent computers to play games that require human skills, such as chess, has come a long way in at least developing specialized skills.

When people think of artificial intelligence, they think of human-like robots that will take over the world. However, that is probably not a realistic viewpoint of its direction, although robots will be used for many applications.

Today, artificial intelligence is accepted as a computer structure that can learn and make decisions and judgments, all in a humanlike fashion. They should be adaptable. Experts have also suggested they should show intelligence and be able to have intention. That last one is hard to quantify in real terms of saying what "intent" is, but for practical purposes, AI systems can make decisions without human input.

AI systems can use machine learning, but they also use other ways to learn, including rules-based behavior and deep learning. Machine learning can be incorporated into an AI system, but an AI system can be built that does not use machine learning.

Narrow AI

Most applications of artificial intelligence will be considered "narrow AI." That is a computer system designed to think like a human, but only for a narrow, specific task. An example of this is the IBM computer Deep Blue that played chess. Other narrow AI systems are being developed, and several are already in use, such as Siri and Alexa, and self-driving cars. Narrow AI relies on machine learning or deep learning. The ability to use these methods of learning allow engineers to create computer systems for a specific task without having to develop very large computer programs with huge numbers of lines of code.

Deep learning is learning that is done with multi-layered neural networks. Inputs are weighted as the system learns, and connections between nodes are strengthened. The multi-layered systems used with deep learning are said to be "hidden" because they will interact with other nodes in the system, but not with the outside world through inputs and outputs.

General AI

General AI involves developing a general artificially intelligent system that can completely mimic the intelligence of a human being. This is more like the androids of Hollywood fame that people think about when they hear the term "artificial intelligence." This is a very difficult problem to solve, and progress in this area has been slow. To be sure that the concept is understood, in this case, you would have a generally intelligent system that could learn and do anything. This is quite different from building an intelligent system that can play chess and approve or deny a loan application.

Big Data and Artificial Intelligence

Right now, the relationship between big data and artificial intelligence is focused on narrow AI. You can think of big data as information and artificial intelligence as the brain. Big data feeds artificially intelligent systems.

Big data is raw data input for AI. Think about artificial intelligence in the same way that a child learns in school. The child is exposed to a large amount of data over the course of their schooling. Big data is the same way. This is the data provided as learning material for artificially intelligent systems. This allows the AI system to learn so it can work independently later, the same way that a medical student learns while in medical school and then works as an independent doctor after finishing their training. Think of big data as the lectures and books that the student reads and follows to learn their craft.

AI systems are adaptive computing systems. When they see new data, they adapt to it and can modify their own behavior once they have been trained. Big data by itself is dumb. It is just a collection of information, and when presented as a raw data set, no intelligence is associated with that information until it can be analyzed. It can include text, numerical data, photographs, videos, you name it. By itself, it is nothing more than that. Big data can be processed, which means it will be fed to an AI system to detect the patterns and relationships that may exist in the data.

Without big data, AI, as it is currently used, would be completely worthless. AI systems need big data to learn the skills they are expected to have. At the same time, we can say that big data would have no value without AI and, in particular, without machine learning. Without these tools, it would not be possible to detect the patterns inherent in the data. Collections of data would be taking up space on hard drives all over the world but not be very useful.

To learn effectively, artificially intelligent systems must have the proper amount of data. The more data that an AI system can examine, the more accurate it will be when deployed on its own. This fact alone means that artificial intelligence and big data are closely linked together. Before the era of big data, progress in artificial intelligence was slow and spotty. Now it is proceeding at a rapid pace. You can think of big data as the food that artificial intelligence needs to grow and blossom. Without that food, artificial intelligence will slow and stagnate. This is why the relationship between big data and artificial intelligence is important and long-lasting.

As we have seen, artificially intelligent systems are used with big data to solve many problems. This includes anomaly detection, where an artificially intelligent system that has been trained on big data can then look at new data coming in real time and determine whether fraud exists, for example.

Artificial intelligence can also help big data scientists by showing them patterns in the data they did not know were there, and it can also be used to do important work such as Bayesian analysis and graph theory. An example of Bayesian analysis is predicting the future behavior of a customer given their past behavior, or the past behavior of other customers with similar characteristics.

In short, big data and artificial intelligence are used in an integrated way. Artificial intelligence is the brains of the operation, but big data is used to train the system.

Chapter 9: Business Intelligence

Quite simply, business intelligence refers to the technologies used to collect and analyze business information. The purpose of business intelligence is to improve the functioning of the business and provide better products and services to the public while cutting down on the costs associated with doing business. Many of the tools described in this book will be used as a part of business intelligence. For example, you will be using data mining, and other techniques used to study and analyze data are also important. Business intelligence is an overarching theme, where the ultimate meaning and direction from all the data that a business has can be integrated into one coherent whole.

Data Analysis

At its core, intelligence is data analysis of business information. This can include reporting, processing, data mining, and predictive analytics. The results of business intelligence can be used to make decisions across the levels of the business, including setting future goals, improving customer service, or developing new products.

At the center of business intelligence is the concept of integration. This is where the term "intelligence" comes from. All the business data available to the enterprise is fully integrated into a useful whole that can, in turn, be used to set a strategic direction for the business. This will help the business gain insight into new markets, launching new products, and the productivity of advertising and marketing efforts.

Big Data and Business Intelligence

Big data is at the heart of business intelligence. To generate business intelligence, experts have proposed that data gathering, data storage, and knowledge form its core. As you can see from this definition, big data, combined with other aspects such as data mining, predictive analytics, and machine learning, is what leads to business intelligence. To have solid knowledge management, it will be necessary to discover patterns and relationships that exist in the data available to the company.

Business intelligence will use big data in a myriad of ways. Unstructured data can be an important component, and it must be analyzed to be useful to the company. Business intelligence can be used for forecasts, budgeting, and other activities. Statistical models will also be developed, and they will be trained using the big data that the company has access to.

One way business intelligence will leverage big data is through the internal data the corporation possesses. This internal data will include memos, emails, notes, charts, reports, meeting notes, presentations, images, marketing material, and information from customer support. This information is typically unstructured or semi-structured. The company will tend to have a smaller amount of structured data.

The goal is to use this data to get the company operating in a more efficient manner. Essentially, the company has its own internal big data, which can be managed using the standard tools described elsewhere in this book. One goal of business intelligence is to make it easier for employees to access and use this information, which is difficult to do when it is in an unstructured form. Businesses may collect metadata on elements of the unstructured data in their possession and then use that in a relational database to create a semi-structured data set.

Business management may also be interested in any patterns, relationships, and trends that may be present in this data. They may want to incorporate machine learning and analysis to extract those trends and use them to improve the operation of the company.

Patterns in the data, especially related to emails and meeting notes and other recorded conversations, can be used to enhance and improve collaboration and communication throughout the organization. To make the best decisions, the tools available for analysis, such as data mining, statistical analysis, and predictive or prescriptive analytics, can be applied to the big data in the company's possession. Machine learning is increasingly playing an important role in these processes.

Over time, the ability to get a better handle over large amounts of internal data will help companies run far more efficiently. This will improve collaboration and make communication more effective, timely, and productive.

The field of business intelligence is rapidly developing and offers opportunities for consulting work and for direct work. It is estimated that around $20 billion a year is being spent on business intelligence already. Business intelligence experts can help companies manage their internal big data and use the right machine learning to get the information they need from the data.

Chapter 10: Data Analytics

Data analytics is used by businesses to analyze data and draw conclusions from the information contained in the data. This is to help companies make more informed business decisions. Data analytics can also have broad applications outside the business world. In the context of business, it is sometimes referred to as business analytics.

What Is Data Analytics Used For?

Business analytics has a broad spectrum of application. At the very core, you can say that data analytics is used to help a business operate in a more efficient and productive manner. The central goal is to improve business performance, and this can happen in a wide variety of ways. For example, improving customer service may be one goal of data analytics. Increasing revenues and profits are also important uses.

It can also be used to study emerging markets and analyze the competition. In short, data analytics can operate in any area where data can be processed. In the exploratory phase, the goal is to go through data and search for patterns and relationships in the data. Hopefully by now, this sounds a bit familiar.

Business leaders who are doing the analysis can make hypotheses about the data, and while doing exploratory data analytics, there will be an effort to determine if the hypotheses are true or false.

Types of Data Used

Data analytics works with quantitative and qualitative data. Qualitative data will be any non-numerical data and could include emails, text messages, call recordings, images, video, and audio. The data sets used can include both structured and unstructured data.

More Advanced Techniques

The process of data analytics is evolving, and more advanced methods of data analysis are being used more now than in the past. This includes data mining, predictive analytics, and machine learning. The data used for data analytics can, therefore, be understood to be big data. The data sets will be used in the standard ways to seek out previously unknown patterns and trends in the data.

Applications of Data Analytics

One area where data analytics is frequently used is in the prevention of fraud and theft by banks. In particular, patterns of spending and money withdrawal can be used to estimate whether a debit card has been stolen and is being used by the criminal. To use this type of information and make such determinations, the banks have used the big data gathered on previous incidents of theft, where spending and withdrawal patterns were detected using machine learning.

Data analytics can be used in any application that involves patterns of that nature. For example, it can be applied to any business that relies on a subscription service. The analysis can use the big data from previous customer defections to detect patterns in current data that could indicate a customer is thinking of leaving the company.

Data analytics is frequently used to improve the efficiency of internal company operations. One area where this is often done is in manufacturing. Using data analytics, the company can help improve staffing, distribute workloads more efficiently, and plan ahead when increased demand requires more output.

One interesting application in data analytics is in video and casino gaming to keep players engaged with a game for a long period. This is done using past data about the distribution of rewards at the right rate. Studies of this data go back decades, where data was collected via slot machines in casinos. This type of information is used in modern video games to bring them to a level of frustration while playing the game, and then give them rewards at the right moment to keep them interested.

Such applications are wide and varied. Data analytics is simply analyzing the raw data a company has access to about customer behavior, internal company operations, and so forth. Over the years, the processes used with data analytics have been automated to make data more suitable for human use, helping businesses become more efficient.

Conclusion

Thank you for taking the time to read this exciting book about big data. I'd like to conclude by talking a bit about the implications of the big data revolution we are experiencing. There are two main threads that fit into this discussion. The first one is the possibility of massive job losses and upheaval of the economy as a result of these new technologies. The second thread involves privacy issues.

When we think about new technology, we tend to think in terms of gadgets. The first thing that might come to mind is your cell phone. Self-driving cars, spaceflight, and other technologies that you can hold in your hand or see also intrigue us.

For this reason, big data is an unusual development in the history of technology. It is largely unseen by the general public even though you are feeling its effects. Also, in the process of analyzing big data, there are analysts, statistical models, fast computer systems, along with a large computer storage systems and cloud computing. If people think about it at all, they would probably be focused on the computers themselves. However, it is the data on the hard drives and the software algorithms that analyze that data which is important.

When you consider all the technologies that have been developed in the last fifty years, many of them pale in significance compared to big data. For example, think of all the attention that has been lavished on cell phones. For all the wonder that a device like an iPhone provides, its impact on society at large won't be near the impact from big data and machine learning.

For example, a smartphone is unlikely to cause you to lose your job. However, big data in machine learning may do exactly that. Whether that matters to you, one thing we know for certain is that possibly millions of jobs will be eliminated over a very short time. It is too early to determine what the impact of this will be. As I have mentioned before, we can look to previous history for some idea of what might be coming. In several instances in the past, new technologies have created far more jobs than they destroyed. In fact, that has always been the case ever since the Industrial Revolution started. We already talked about the example of the textile machines and the Luddites, but there are even more recent examples. Those under the age of forty probably are not aware of what life was like prior to the massive adoption of computer systems. In the 1970s and even into the 1980s, many businesses did spreadsheet work by hand. Secretaries were used to typing documents on typewriters.

At that time, spreadsheet programs and word processors we are rapidly gaining the market share as businesses adopted them. This scared many people at the time. People imagined that the office would soon become free of paper and that the advent of spreadsheets and word processors would eliminate millions of jobs.

The same thing happened the more these technologies became used in more and more offices. Rather than eliminate jobs, the impact was to create millions of new jobs instead. This happens because productivity is massively increased with each introduction of new technology. Second, it frees people from trivial tasks they were devoting their time to before. A strange thing happens as these patterns develop. People find out that new must-do and must-have things become required in the new economy that springs out of the chaos.

That is likely to be the case this time as well. Although robotics will certainly eliminate many jobs, new jobs that you cannot even imagine right now will spring up in their place. Some people cite the rapid pace of transformation as a reason to be pessimistic about this. However, it should be noted that this will also cause an explosion in the pace of change, which brings about an entirely new business in place of the old jobs lost to robotics and artificial intelligence.

Another thing that happens during a transformation process like this is that the economy itself grows by a large amount, so even if you lost a certain number of jobs, the growth of the economy, which is benefiting from the new technologies, will more than offset the loss of those jobs. There will always be jobs for humans to perform, so people might be doing new things, but they will certainly have some things to do.

In fact, we are already seeing this on a large-scale. When the internet became available to the general public and to businesses, it created many new jobs and job categories that did not exist before. This was also accompanied by changes generated by the existence of software programs such as Photoshop. Some new job categories that have proven very lucrative include web programmers, graphic designers, JavaScript programmers, and so forth. This has also happened with respect to mobile or smartphones. It is estimated that as a result of the iPhone, there are 1.5 million new jobs in the United States. These jobs are related to app development and include computer programming jobs, user interface design, graphic design, as well as millions of people who have started their own businesses centered on developing iPhone apps. The numbers are probably even larger when you consider Google's Android.

In addition, the video gaming industry is growing in leaps and bounds. Games continue to be developed for traditional devices like consoles, but many companies are only developing games for use on smartphones. This has created an entirely new set of job possibilities. In my view, something similar will happen as artificial intelligence, big data, and machine learning continue to weave their way throughout our society.

Regarding the privacy issue, privacy and ethical concerns are certainly important. However, it is my opinion that big data has already won the day and won't go away anytime soon. In fact, the importance of big data will increase in the coming years, and its commercial impact is too large for companies to ignore. Not only does selling data provide a lucrative way to generate income, but big data also increases the power of marketing and advertising as well as customer service for large corporations. The benefits of this are just way too large, and no matter what politicians do, I don't believe they can stop this process.

With that in mind, we must consider protecting our own data, becoming more aware of the terms of service and privacy rules, and being more concerned about security. One factor that has made data sharing controversial is a simple fact people do not pay attention to. It is painful, but you must take the time to read software company documents regarding privacy. If Congress will do anything, it might be helpful if they would require companies to present clear and easy-to-understand information related to these issues that could be read quickly by customers. Think about what happens nine times out of ten when people open a website or app and are faced with terms of service or privacy agreements. Most people are far too impatient to deal with this, and the legalese of these documents simply gives them a headache. So they quickly dismiss the document by agreeing to it. If you are engaging in that type of behavior, you cannot blame Facebook, Google, or any of the other big tech companies if you find out later that your data was shared.

Politicians are probably mistaken if they believe they will solve this problem by breaking up the big tech companies. Big data will still be there, and it will be worth more than ever if that happens. In my opinion, it is probably better to have a few powerful companies managing and controlling a large fraction of the data. In any case, if they break up these companies, the problem will just shift around rather than go away. It might also be harder for governments to regulate, which would defeat their purpose. I tend to take a libertarian view as long as there is not abuse, so in my opinion, the company should not be broken up. However, there should be some simple regulations put in place to ensure that people can protect their privacy. Data sharing should be allowed, but no one should be able to identify specific individuals in that data.

I would like to thank you again for reading this book, and I hope you have found it educational, informative, and useful. If it has proven to be productive for you, please feel free to leave a review.